WOMAN TO WOMAN

STRAIGHT TO THE POINT

Dr. Cierrah Perrin, Ed.D

ISBN 13: 978-0-9996477-0-7

I would like to dedicate this book to my number one woman, my mother, *S. Denise Yarber.*

Your strength, your guidance, your pain, your challenges, your grace, and faith have all helped me learn and grow.

I'll always be your "Fatty."

This one is for you lady!

Table of Contents

Foreword

Women, we are indeed one of God's most powerful and complex creatures. There is nothing on the planet more complex than a woman. We are multi-dimensional beings and have been given the incredible ability to be the conduit through which life manifests into the physical state. Now I say this because it does not have anything to do with the obvious physical manifestation of life, such as bearing children, but more so our innate ability to breathe life into our loved ones, our jobs, our studies, our passions, our lovers, our husbands, and for current purposes, ourselves.

As women, we are always simultaneously experiencing an onslaught of emotions while trying to process our daily personal struggles and keep up the facade that we have it all together. For example, we can be happy to have gained a promotion, but emotionally distraught over a breakup, worried about a parent, trying to nurture a child, or just feeling inadequate for not having one. In some cases, we can simply be trying to stay the hell away from even the mere suggestion of having to add yet another responsibility to the growing list of tasks society puts on us. Not to mention the pressure we put on ourselves. We have to always be pretty, and classy, be seen and not heard, etc. All these hats, whether or not we desire to wear them, we have on all at once.

It's exhausting to be so much to so many, and that's where this little gem comes in handy. This book is not your everyday read that you store on your coffee table and let collect dust. This book is that "get your life" conversation that you have with that one girlfriend that always tells you the truth. You know it's gonna be ugly, and she knows it's gonna hurt, but the truth is just as righteous as it is productive. After you hear it, you are no longer satisfied wallowing in your issue, but because someone has peered into your soul and read you for filth, you have to act and begin to move in a more positive direction.

No matter where you are on your journey, there is something in here for you. We are already our own worst critics, not only dealing with all of our complexities, but also trying to help people understand and respect us. This book is the detox we need for our souls. Our spirit is where the healing needs to take place, so we can vent and have an avenue to go out there and be great. Every day, there is a lesson to be learned, and that is why this is a very practical push in the right direction to embracing your purpose.

I will never forget the day I met Dr. Cierrah Perrin. She was just a student fresh out of law school—beautiful, statuesque, and extremely organized. She told me she had been looking for a stylist and had, as a matter of fact, come across my info while in another state, but for reasons unknown, she had not booked. Now here she was, sitting in my chair looking bright-eyed and bushy-tailed to the naked eye, but completely emotionally drained. I started on her hair, and she started giving me the rundown on her current state. She had just finished law school and was down to her last few bucks; her savings were low, and it had been difficult to find a job. In that moment, she said she felt like giving up and going back home may have to be a viable option. She just couldn't fathom how she would make it through this trial.

Here she was in a new city, with no family, and loved ones back home who depended on her. I heard something in her voice that I was all too familiar with. All of us have it. It's the will to keep fighting even when it seems you have reached the brink of despair, and the extinction of hope feels imminent. In these valleys of life, sometimes all we need is a reminder or a word to encourage us. It is the place where your heart is weary, but a few words will ignite your mind and give you the wherewithal you need to push past the pain. I remember telling her that day that I was her family now. I meant every word. The funny thing is, she thought she was the only one with a need, but I saw what she could be, and I knew I needed her. I was raising a daughter that needed a tangible role model besides myself. I saw in her what I so often saw in many women that had sat in that very same place and poured their hearts out to me. I saw the turmoil in her eyes. We prayed, and I told her that from that day forward, I was going to speak the future I saw for her into existence. I told her I was renaming her Dr. Cee. She laughed through the tears, and I programmed it in my phone as such. Fast-forward to a few years later, and my sister and friend were walking across a stage, accepting her doctorate degree! She never let me forget that I was the first one who believed in her and called her that. That's not to say that it was easy. There were many rough patches along the way, but when she could not walk through a door, she found a window, and when there was no window, she knocked down a wall. Now she has taken it a step further by building houses with doors, windows, and tools to teach you how to break forth and not give up.

This is not another "make me feel inspired to do better, and then tomorrow when the magic wears off, I'll do even less" message. This is a practical conversation between women that will indeed inspire you, but also unlock the enigma that plagues us all: How? How do you move forward when you are tired, broken, frustrated, confused, or hurt? How do you not give up when every single situation presents as if throwing in the towel is your only option?

I'll tell you: You deal with life's hiccups the same way you would eat an elephant. As it is said, you don't try to devour the elephant all at once; you evaluate how much you can eat at each interval and take one bite at a time. It may take a little longer, it may not be as glamorous as social media personalities make it seem, but trust me, before you know it, that elephant will be a testimony and no longer a test. I pray that this book caresses the very soul of every eye reading it, and give you the uplift and kick in the pants you need to be exactly what you were born to be! I pray that it will provoke conversations and self-discovery and women will support each other and not tear each other down. We don't need to do it to each other; society already does a helluva job. I pray that by the time you finish, there will be several checks off your checklist and you will be closer to your dreams. Last but not least, I pray that the love that was put into writing this jewel will be felt deep in your heart, will resonate in your soul, and will be reciprocated through the great works of your mind, beloved.

Joy C. Stewart

Life Coach and Spiritual Advisor

Day 1
Start Somewhere.

Every 24 hours, we have an opportunity to get our sh*t together. Don't depend on the 365th day of every year to change your life. Each day requires discipline. Change is not instantaneous. It demands constant attention. If you are uncomfortable with yourself, your energy will die, and it will become visible to others. To prevent this from occurring, you must do something that makes you feel good and kill the negativity from your perception of yourself. Some days, you just have to create your own sunshine.

We have become so used to seeing the result of people winning materialistically, we have no idea that winning spiritually precedes it. Self- love isn't just bubble baths and face masks, it's owning up to your sh*t and accepting your flaws, encouraging yourself to do better. How many times have you looked in the mirror and did not like who you saw? Do not be surprised, many women have felt this way, at some point in their lives -- and whether it is the pressure of career, motherhood, being a wife, being single, or just life that is wearing you down, it is important that you do a self-checkup. When you feel this way, you must remind yourself that self-love is under constant construction.

It is essential that you know you are beautiful just the way you are irrespective of the standard the society classified as beautiful. It is important that you rediscover your unique beauty because that is the only way you can stand out. Instead of allowing life to get you down, do something that makes you feel good to shift that energy. Each time you look at the mirror, find beauty from within. So, when you wake up on a morning and nothing seem to be going right and you just aren't feeling yourself, instead of getting depressed about it, reflect on the ingredients that make you uniquely special, i.e. all the good qualities you possess. Remind yourself, check yourself.

Constantly remind yourself of how far you've come, instead of focusing on how further you have to go. Always find a release in the days of self-doubt, whether it is yoga, singing your favorite song, dancing to the beat of your favorite song, meditation, etc. Many times, we fall victim to superficial beauty. Seeing women with long hair in magazines and makeup crew that beautify them each day is ideal, but not realistic. It is not my intention to degrade the celebrities or models that have this luxury, but to make women realize that intrinsic beauty sustains the body, spirit and soul. Extrinsic perception of beauty is a temporary gratification of the mind. Which would you rather have?

> **Woman to Woman:** There was a time in my life when I thought that I had to reduce who I was for others to be comfortable in my presence. By doing this, I took something away from myself that made me feel incomplete and less beautiful. See, I had to learn that everyone is not going to embrace me. Just because you have a lot of people in the audience does not mean they are fans. Some are critics, while others are spectators, waiting for you to break down. I learned that true beauty comes from within. Self-love cannot be measured according to the fallacies of life. Feeling good in my skin supersedes any amount of satisfaction that I am yet to reach. It is important that every woman recognizes the importance of inner-beauty before diverting love to anyone else.

QUOTE OF THE DAY:

The beauty of a woman is not in a facial mode but the true beauty in a woman is reflected in her soul. It is the caring that she lovingly gives, the passion that she shows. The beauty of a woman grows with the passing years.

– Audrey Hepburn

Day 2

If You Correct The Cause, The Condition Will Go Away.

People can be so invested in you but aren't investing in you. Good relationships just don't happen. They demand effort, prayer, love, patience, and two people willing to get through hard times. There is only one thing more precious than our time and that is who we spend it with. You change for two reasons: either you learn enough that you want to, or you have been hurt enough that you have no other choice. At some point in your life, you are going to have to demand what you deserve and be willing to walk away if what you require can't be provided. Dig deep and become in tune with yourself. Some won't know how to deal with it because the deeper you become, the more truth you reveal. And the truth scares the hell out of some people. Don't try to change anyone, just simply change how you deal with them.

Take inventory and see whose expiration date has passed. Cut the poison out of your life. No matter what or whom it may be. It is very imperative to make sure that there is no dead weight weighing you down. Often, we are afraid to take inventory in our lives to see who no longer serves a purpose. The very person beside you that appears to be helping you row the boat could be secretly causing it to sink. There comes the point in your life when you must re-evaluate priorities and take accountability. This means that you must go down the list of the people in your life to see if he or she is a hindrance to your personal growth. I believe there are certain seasons that particular people are supposed to be in one's life. However, I too have made the mistake of having lifetime expectations for people with seasonal roles. After realizing that this mistake was hurting me, I came to the point that I realized who was significant; realizing who was a blessing and who was simply a life lesson. The process wasn't easy. It's hard to disassociate yourself from people who are familiar, but it is very critical for your growth.

People who are blessings always have your best interest in mind. These are the people who know you best and who want the best results for your life. They will never use your weakest moments against you. Their relationships do not come with conditions. We as humans have a habit of associating longevity and expectancy. One should have neither to do with the other. Just because a person has been around for years does not mean that they have your best interest in mind. However, we habitually intertwine length of friendships with significance. I am not advocating the notion of giving up on people who have been there for you. On the other hand, you have to be accountable for those who you are allowing to perpetuate their way via your life. These are the very people that you constantly find yourself doubting. If you doubt the character of a person, usually that person is a seasonal entity in your life, only existing to make you learn valuable lessons. Being aware of others' character is a huge benefit in avoiding the turmoil of life. So, ask yourself, who is a blessing and who is around for a lesson? The biggest mistake you can make is allowing someone who no longer deserves to be in your life to remain so. When you start to find yourself, you'll begin to lose the thing that kept you lost. You can never change what you don't confront.

Woman to Woman: I look back at a relationship with someone who was in my life for years. I mean she was my very best friend. We met in college and had so much in common. She and I did everything together. We laughed, we cried, we traveled, we got our hearts broken, we got through hard times. I thought our bond was unbreakable. For sure, she was going to be in my life forever, right? We talked about how we would be one another's maid-of-honors in our weddings and give our future children one another's names. Sad to say, she and I have not spoken in years. We had one argument and we literally stopped being friends. It wasn't until later on in life that I realized that we were never really friends. Or at least, she wasn't the same type of friend to me as I were to her. It would be great to give you a tear-jerker on how she and I reunited, right? Sorry ladies, that is not the reality in which we live. Now I tried to repair the friendship in the way that I saw fit, but it was so very hard. It was like attempting to put on a size 6 shoe, and I am a size 7.5. The truth was that she and I did not fit in one another's life anymore. It was a very heartbreaking situation for me, but I confused longevity with sincerity. Looking back, I see that we shared commonalities, but the genuine love and regard that I had for our friendship was never truly reciprocated. Thus, I had to take accountability and inventory in my life.

QUOTE OF THE DAY:

I've learned that people will forget what you said, people will forget what you did, but people will never forget how you made them feel.

– Maya Angelou

Day 3

God Disrupts Your Entire Life To Talk To You.

Do you ever wish God would just walk into your room and sit on the bed and say, "Okay, this is what you should do?" The woman you are becoming will cost you relationships, spaces, and material things. Choose her over everything. Pain is certain; suffering is optional. I always remember that old saying, "no one said it would be easy." Whoever stated that first was right; no one said it would be easy. No one said that things would always work out. No one said that you would not cry, that you would not have bad days, and you would go through life with everything copacetic. However, we all come from different walks of life, some worse than others. Many women have endured abuse, been violated in ways that are unimaginable, even lost parents at an early age or been the product of a bad environment. It is important that you give time back to yourself after you have given it to so many others.

The societal view is that troubled young girls usually end up as troubled women. This is only true when your past is a constant factor in your present. I can recall one of the worst times in my life. My parents' divorce was something that I had trouble with for a long time. It came to a point where I did not believe in the power of love because I asked myself how something that I was taught to believe in could fail me. In this state of mind, I was miserable; I was upset all the time and just in anguish from the result of my parents' divorce. If you noticed, I said, "I" meaning the way I felt was in a bad state; affecting MY life. I know that pain is a powerful emotion, especially when it has been endured for such a long period, or practically your whole life because you were just a victim of your circumstances. However, you cannot allow what has happened in your past to cripple your future. There comes a time in one's life where you just have to let go and heal. I, personally being a believer in God, turned to prayer and spiritual guidance to get through one of the most painful experiences in my life to date. I prayed for strength, I prayed and asked that God allow me to forgive my parents and believe in love again. I prayed for guidance and was led to a great therapist. I realized that hanging on to pain was not healthy and it was tainting my future, my mental state, and my spirit. Under no circumstance am I implying not to deal with the issues that are causing you pain just by pretending that it did not happen. However, what I am saying is to find a healthy release to make you generate positive energy in addressing the worst times in your life. It's so empowering to say, "this no longer serves me" and walk away in peace.

There is nothing wrong with turning to professional counseling or therapy to help you heal or understand your emotions. When your past is hard to deal with, and you find it jeopardizing your future, it is important that you find out the best way to heal. Consider yourself a survivor; you have survived a painful experience, and you possess a paramount of strength to have come out of whatever circumstances that attempted to conquer you. Remember that true happiness is never found; it is created within. Your daily performance reflects your deepest beliefs. In tough times, we always gain something. We may not like it, but we gain experience, endurance, and our character continues to develop. If you wait for someone to heal you, you'll have a tormented life. Learn to restore yourself from within.

> **Woman to Woman:** As I mentioned, my parents' divorce was probably one of the most painful experiences to date. You would think that it happened in my adolescence; however, it happened in my adulthood. I often wonder if witnessing it

in my childhood would have been less painful. Watching my mother broken down with no regard was very painful. I was angry at my father, which caused me not to speak to him for years to come. I was mad at him for not fighting for our family, for instilling something in us that he did not follow through with himself. During the years of not speaking to my dad, I was most miserable. I was unhappy within. I was embarrassed about how he left us, my mother—his family. It took a lot of prayers, many talks with God, and therapy, for me to forgive him. However, I must admit, I am still a work in progress. However, I could not allow my heart to be paralyzed by one event. I could not allow my father's actions to dictate my outlook on love. I chose to forgive; I chose to move on, I chose to take control. Once I fully committed to healing, I started to understand that sometimes, people are instruments to aide in my evolution. I started to focus on the lesson, not the person.

QUOTE OF THE DAY:

No experience is wasted. Everything in life is happening to grow you up, to fill you up, to help you become more of who you were created to be.

– Oprah Winfrey

Day 4

Your Future Self Is Still Waiting On You To Arrive.

Do not look for perfection; just be grateful for staying in a state of progression. Perfection is a disillusioned perception. Searching for perfection will continuously leave one disappointed. Perfection is non-existent, but if you are exploring the option to progress continuously, your view is in a more realistic state. Even those at their best are not perfect. Trusting in the fact that one day, you will someday reach a point of perfection is a misguided fact. You must understand that living is an everyday job. Some days, you have it all together, other days, you can't find your keys sitting on the table right in front of you. See, that's just the expectancies of life, it's ever-changing. Then you have progression. Progression is a state that leads us always desiring to become better. No matter what direction in which you aim, whether it is personally or professionally, it makes you a better individual.

Accepting the fact that you cannot be perfect and that no one is, is a vital stepping stone to experience that keeps you learning and growing throughout womanhood. There is no time not to do what you believe in. The caliber of your thinking delivers the quality of your performance. Never be defined by your past. It was just a lesson, not a life sentence. Your life is the total sum of the decisions that you make every day. If you want to be successful, you must set priorities for yourself. Life is a journey; don't be in such a hurry. Don't be afraid to grow, end bad habits, leave dead-end jobs, cut off unhealthy relationships. Take the initiative. Do not be so hard on yourself when you fall short of what you say you are all about; it happens. Discipline is the key to growth and learning oneself is a better teacher than anything. Through trial and error, you learn to become the best woman you can be. Experience is the best teacher, though the tuition is high. Progress in the midst of it all. The wall does not come before laying the bricks. You lay the bricks one by one to create the wall. Greatness is a building process. Having control of your destiny and living a positive life that promotes progression is the biggest gift that you not only give yourself but to others around you as well.

Your accomplishments often affect those around you. Many of us do not realize that we possess a unique power of individuality. There is always someone paying attention to us, holding admiration. People who look at us like this do not expect for us to be perfect, but just to be ourselves which seemingly becomes an inspiration for them. No decision will pay off more than prioritizing your life and giving extreme focus and energy to things that make you most happy and have the highest return, peace.

> **Woman to Woman:** For a long time, I struggled with the illusion of thinking that I could maintain the demeanor of being so strong all the time. I never wanted anyone to see me weak or vulnerable. Many things attributed to my disposition. Because I had created this insurmountable strength, everyone always assumed I was okay, even when I was not. There were times in my life when I needed a shoulder to cry on, but I would not allow my pride to allude to such exposure. Thus, for a long time, I went through the distress of experiencing things alone. Not because no one wanted to be there, but I exuded a false perception of the mastery of strength. I learned that it is not about always being strong, but more about how to be better.

QUOTE OF THE DAY:

I am learning every day to allow the space between where I am and where I want to be, to inspire me and not terrify me.

– Traci Ellis Ross

Day 5

Don't Sacrifice Being Valuable Just To Be Visible.

You have a choice: be a stand-up woman or have a seat. Too many of us are starting to take pride in being deceitful, conniving, or savage. We've gotten away from wanting to be a good woman and have become enthusiastic about women doing other women dirty rather than doing right by one another. It's like we are at a point where it's so easy for us to sacrifice our character for money or attention. It's becoming the norm to think the only way that you can get ahead is by stepping on someone else; and the only way to keep your feelings and emotions in check is to act like you don't give a damn. Know that you can still be whatever and be a good woman. Keep evolving as long as the world is revolving.

When you finally reach a point where you have your moral, priorities, goals, and aspirations in sync; do not drift back to old habits or people that you let go. Retrograde is a state of movement only meant for planets. You are being presented with a choice: evolve or remain. If you choose to remain unchanged, you will be presented with the same challenges, the same routines, the same storms and circumstances until you learn from them. If you choose to evolve, you will connect with your inner super power, your strength. As women, when we tap into something that we once let go, it compares to reopening a healed womb. Thus, it is imperative that you are consistent with who you are and where you stand. In order to continuously prosper, you must stand firm on what you believe in and who you are as a woman. Constantly going back and forth with things and people who serve you no good is a pure waste of your time and will keep you stagnant. Make peace with your past, and allow that peace to lead you to a brighter future. No one will respect you if you cannot make up your mind on who you are. If you do not know who you are, how do you expect other people to figure it out? It takes a lifetime to learn oneself fully; however, you must establish a starting point on where you can start directing your life in a way which is beneficial to you. Life is such a great tool to keep on learning more and more about who we are; we dictate the people whom we deal with, and most importantly, our purpose.

Believing in oneself is the most important thing. Do not allow anything to make you doubt who you are. You know you are better than anyone else. The direction of your life is dependent on your decisions as a woman. Figure out who you are and start making moves to accomplish everything that you aspire to do or become. Be disciplined about what you respond and react to; not everyone or everything deserves your time, energy, and attention. Shake off what didn't work out. Shake off what somebody told you that you couldn't do. They don't determine your destiny, that's contingent on you.

As you grow and develop into the woman you were meant to be, at times, you may feel like you're losing it. However, you're not losing it, you're getting rid of the old you and manifesting all that comes with the new you. Negativity can only affect you if you are on the same frequency. Vibrate higher. Make a habit of shutting down conversations that involve hating on other people. If you ever can be better, do just that. We all make choices, but in the end, our choices make us who we are. Take care of the ordinary responsibilities and you won't need extraordinary measures to become visible.

Woman to Woman: I have been blessed to have many aunts in my life. Thus, I have viewed the personality traits and characteristics of many different women. I have seen it all, the passive, the aggressive, the volatile, the addict, the passive, and the submissive. At a young age, I started to realize what I wanted to stand for, what my signature would signify. It would be a blatant lie if I stated that I have it all figured out. I learn something new about myself every day. Yet, I know my limitations, I know what I believe in; I know where my morale stands, and I trust that I can accomplish anything to which I dedicate myself. Years ago, my dad told me that I was not born with a silver spoon in my mouth. My response to him was that I know that I was not, nonetheless, where I'm going has nothing to do with where I come from; my destiny is in my hands. I had to reiterate that my life is contingent upon my actions. I know where I stand on my goals and aspirations; I know who I am as a woman presently and the woman I want to grow to be. At that moment, I stood for what I believed in; I did not choose to take a seat. Each phase of my life reveals something new about myself that I was not aware.

QUOTE OF THE DAY:

You can do one of two things; just shut up, which is something I don't find easy, or learn an awful lot very fast, which is what I tried to do.

– Jane Fonda

Reader's Reflection:

Day 6

Stay Committed To Your Decision But Flexible To Your Approach.

Now that you have your goals lined up, you constantly ask yourself, *what if?* What if things do not work out? What if I never accomplish what I dreamed I would? I will not sit here and tell you to stay bogged down with something that is not working out. However, you must make practical goals and act realistically to accomplish those goals. Things may not always work out how you have planned, on the other hand, if you are working towards something that you feel passionately about, do all that you must to see that those goals are completed in the best way you know how. The caliber of your thinking delivers the quality of your performance.

There is no time not to do what you believe in, and follow your passion. I truly believe that any desire that is put in your heart can be accomplished when the determination is there. If those goals that you have set forth are not aligning properly or going as planned, continue to stay dedicated to what you want to do, but evaluate other options in which you can still reach those goals by going a different direction. Trust the process but continue to put in the work. Don't have a sense of entitlement that you deserve to be in a certain place or position without work. Many of us are not born with privilege and legacy; it's up to you to create your own. Thus, at the end of the day, when you have put your best foot forward and you have invested all the time, passion, determination, and will-power into something that you aspire to be, and things are not falling into place the way you desire, it is imperative that you stay committed. God of the universe will not allow you to possess a desire in your heart and not provide you with the talent and tools to fulfill it.

Flexibility is essentially the way to knock down the wall that is blocking you from succeeding. Be open to networking and new ideas. Do not be so stubborn in what you want in the way that you want it that you are rejecting actual success and self-sabotaging yourself. Adding one plus one will always equal two, so if you keep on doing what you have always done, you will get the same results. Keep an open mind; you can never lose by trying and strategizing. When you can't control what's happening, challenge yourself to control the way you respond to what's happening. For that shows your true flexibility in your approach. Your goals are only alive when they show up in your daily activities. Success is not an event; it's the result of your daily habits.

> **Woman to Woman:** What a perfect world we would live in if life came with directions. If only things were that simple, I remember thinking after I completed law school that I was going to come out and immediately fall into a category of the professionally elite. Oh, how naive and misguided I was. My expectations were high; I thought for sure, I cannot accept anything less than what I imagined. But when it came down to me accepting an entry-level job or not being able to provide the necessities for my livelihood—which do you think I chose? Did I settle for less, no, not at all? The truth of the matter is that I needed more experience to get the salary that I envisioned. I did not give up; I just learned how to become flexible to my approach. Thus, that entry-level job led to a promotion, which led to the very experience I needed, which eventually placed me right where I wanted to be. It is critical that you find other ways to get to where you want to be if the intended route or plan is not working for your benefit. If the door closes, you should find a way through the window,

if the window is shut, find a chimney. If the chimney has a fire burning, use the doggy door. No matter your desire or intent, find other approaches that will get you to that same place just in case your plans fall through. For some of us, marriage, kids, or even our careers keep us from fulfilling a desire that we intended. Nevertheless, it is up to you to go get what you truly want. Flexibility is not a negative thing; it allows us to stay on track when our lives take an unexpected turn.

QUOTE OF THE DAY:

Just don't give up trying to do what you really want to do. Where there is love and inspiration, I don't think you can go wrong.

– Ella Fitzgerald

Day 7

Enjoy The Beauty Of Becoming.

Set your goals high enough to inspire you, and low enough to encourage you. If you have something that you want to accomplish, you must be willing to work diligently and take the necessary steps of becoming. Do not have an illusion that you can wake up and just do what you want. Anything worth having is worth working hard for. More than likely, being a woman, you will constantly have to work even harder to prove yourself. The complexities of the female gender entail having a false perception of weakness and not being able to do as well as our male counterparts. As women, we all know this is simply a false dichotomy, but society still seems to support this notion inadvertently. Set your goals high enough to inspire you, and low enough to encourage you. This simply means that you must take it one day at a time and work hard for each and everything that you set out to achieve.

Don't stop when life starts to get a bit uncomfortable. Working hard is a part of life and the truth of the matter is that most of us have to start from the bottom and work our way up. Many of us do not have prominent parents and uncles who own Fortune 500 companies where we can earn a position just because of our last names. Vision is not just a picture of what could be, but a call within to become something more. If you do not work, you will not eat, the world does not owe you anything, so it is entirely up to you to work to provide for yourself. Look for something positive in each day, even if you have to look a little harder some days. What you want to exist, don't settle until you get it. Never trade your integrity for the appearance of success. The secret of your future is hidden in your daily routine.

Diligence is a great tool in encouraging you and determination is essential to inspire you. It takes diligence to master a craft, to go through years of school or to be trained professionally. It takes determination to work a less favorable position in hopes that one day, it will lead to the position in which you seek. You have to put in work to essentially accomplish your goals, if you want it, which is perfectly fine, be willing to do all that it takes to obtain it. If more people put more work behind wants, there would be less "coulda, shoulda, woulda" and more doers. One day, it just clicks. You realize what is important and what isn't. You learn to care less about what others think and love yourself. You realize how far you've come and appreciate your growth. You smile because you are truly proud of yourself and your dedication to your goals unfolding before your eyes.

> **Woman to Woman**: My goal is to write a series of motivational books for women. That is a huge goal that I set for myself. However, I know that I must complete my first book before I can even entertain the thought of a series of books. Thus, I have set my paramount goal of inspiration to sell a series of book, but also a more realistic goal to encourage me, which is first publishing one book. Aligning our goals realistically leads to more advantageous results which are needed to work out any kinks in our plans. There are many components in our lives when we over-think, over-exuberate, and overreact because our expectations of results were misconstrued with actual reality. It is important to always remember that the only way to get to ten is to go through one through nine first.

QUOTE OF THE DAY:

I found that every time I asked for permission, the answer tended to be no, so I had to make my own yeses.

– Issa Rae

Day 8

You Had A Purpose Before Anyone Had An Opinion.

Until purpose is discovered, your existence has no meaning. This may sound harsh. However, the reality is that, so many people are aimlessly wondering this world with no idea why they are here and who they should be. People that are fueled by their purpose rarely check for permission to proceed. Understanding your role and your contribution to the world is internally intimate, it's for you to know and follow up with action. We get in the habit of sharing our good news with the wrong people. As a result, we get negative feedback that deters us from staying committed or taking a course of action.

You cannot allow praise or criticism to get the best of you; it's a weakness to get caught up in either. We are never too certain of what motivates our thoughts. Question yourself, you will save yourself lots of headaches. Be honest with yourself about what truly matters in your life. You can never stop putting in your best because no one is watching or giving you credit. Your defining moment could happen when you least expect it. The difference between who you are and who you want to become is what you do. Don't allow yourself to be motivated by opinions. You have to get so sure of who you are that no one's judgement, rejection, or bad behavior can rock you. Choose your company wisely; not everyone is going in your direction. With better choices, you will see better results.

One day, it has to click that no matter what you do, everyone will have an opinion about how they think your story will end. Everyone isn't meant to be a fan. You can't get obsessed with the achievements or failures of the day. Life is a journey. You are a work in progress and your tomorrow will be better because you're living in your purpose, not for the opinion of others. Want to learn how not to get caught up in opinions? Focus on what to do next instead of worrying about what people will say. Right thinking, based on right believing produces the appropriate results. Where the focus goes, your energy flows.

Woman to Woman: I'm a middle child. I'm an overachiever. Growing up, I grew up with an older sister who was born with Sickle Cell Anemia; a genetic blood disease that causes one to have severe pain. I always thought that because my sister had to get extra attention, due to her illness, that my parents did not care. At an early age, I became very resilient and independent. I wanted my parents to be proud of me. I wanted them to see me. I carried on this state of mind all the way into my late teen years. It wasn't a good feeling living to get praise from a person or people to fulfill yourself. If you never hear it, it can break you. That's not fair, that someone, an outside entity, can destroy something that you worked so hard on—yourself. After having conversations with my parents later in my adult years, I expressed to them the state of mind that I was in as a young teenager, needing their praise, needing them to see me. They were shocked to hear that I felt so isolated from them and the love that they offered. I could release the sense of proving early enough where it didn't do a lot of damage in my adult life. I learned that I had to be true to me regardless of what that looked like to others. Are you still proving? Set your goals. Stay quiet about them. Work your ass off to accomplish them and then clap for yourself. It's about you, no one else.

QUOTE OF THE DAY:

People are like stained-glass windows. They sparkle and shine when the sun is out, but when the darkness sets in, their true beauty is revealed only if there is a light from within.

– Elizabeth Kübler-Ross

Day 9

You Shall Be Compensated For The Work That God Created You To Do, Keep Working.

The two most important days of your life are the day you were born, and the day you figure out why. There are many great people that we will never know about because they lacked something that eventually compromised it all. Work hard and be consistent in delivering results and perfecting your craft to mastery level. I am not promoting the notion to seek fame, but if you want to do it, and you feel passionate about it; master your craft. Put in the work and dedication that it takes to set you apart from others that are in the same field. Do not allow yourself to go to sleep at night knowing that you could have done more. You can't be unproductive through the day knowing that you are trying to get ahead. You can't be lazy knowing someone out there is working harder and smarter than you for the same opportunity. You can't sit back and be okay with mediocrity in your relationship or your activities. Your life is worth more than is expected as typical. Don't let yourself down. You can't do what everyone else is doing if you don't want to end up like everyone else.

The thing about skill and talent, it's uniquely yours. There may be people who do what you do, but they don't possess the same ingredients in which you do. Never think the hustle is beneath you, that's how you fall off. If you want it, you will find a way. If you don't, you will find an excuse. No matter what your craft may be, if you are willing to put your name on it, you should put 150% effort in mastering it on a level that separates you from others. What separates those people that we never heard of from those that became a specialty in her field is the amount of work one puts in what she loves to do. Passion is a strong emotion that allows one to be irrepressible. Find something that you are passionate about and commit to mastering it to the best of your ability. There is a woman that you want to become, and until you reach that point, you have work to do.

It is important that you are willing to master whatever goal it is that you want to accomplish. Just reaching it is good, but becoming a master of something that is conquered makes you special in the way that God or the universe intended you to be. Do all that you can to be all that you want to become. Work harder than most because your desire is greater than many. The door will open as you continue to align your mastery with opportunities. It won't be easy, but it will be worth it. Remember, that we all get our shot. The very desire to find shortcuts makes you eminently unsuited for any kind of mastery.

No one is self-made. We are all products of relationships, circumstances, and influence. Ask yourself, are your relationships cultivating the best circumstances to influence your future? Our actions are usually based on three constraints. The relationships you have with people are a critical component of the direction your life will go. No matter if you were accepted or rejected by people. The very people that you interact with build the circumstances in which you either thrive or remain stagnant. The circumstances in which you were born are out of your control. However, different relationships can aid you in switching gears. You have the final say. Influence from relationships helps shape your reality and perspective.

> **Woman to Woman:** I have always been a visionary. Earlier on, I decided that I wanted to be a certain type of woman and I've been working very hard to become her. I have made a conscious effort to work on myself in every way. I wanted to become a doctor, I worked hard to complete my doctorate degree in Organizational Leadership. I wanted to become a

business owner, so I started Perrin Professional Group. I have always worked hard since I was thirteen to obtain the things I wanted in life. I didn't grow up rich, nor did I grow up poor. However, I always had the sense of wanting more, to see more, to do more. I know that nothing comes from a lazy woman; and if I don't work, I won't eat. However, in that same stance, I know that my quality of food is contingent on my level of work. I want the best things that life has to offer, not because I am superficial or shallow, but because I work hard to obtain things that will make me happy. I'm working hard to position myself so that I can grow from a principal consultant to a director; eventually, an executive role. I'm into information technology as a profession. I work with highly intelligent people in a competitive field. However, I do know that my skills are uniquely mine. Though I may have colleagues that possess the same set or similar skills, they don't have the formula that makes me special. Thus, I will continue to work hard on my craft to strengthen my skills to position myself to get to the next level. Are you working to maintain or working to grow?

QUOTE OF THE DAY:

When I stand before God at the end of my life, I would hope that I would not have a single bit of talent left, and could say, "I used everything you gave me."

– Erma Bombeck

Day 10

You Can't Continue To Explain Yourself To People Who Are Committed To Misunderstanding You.

Stop breaking your own heart by exaggerating your place in other people's lives. You aren't free until you have no need to impress anyone. If you are doing all that you can and the goals that you have set forth for yourself are in motion, don't allow bitter Betty to come take that away from you. Now, you remember all the naysayers that wished you badly. It is not a good idea to exploit your accomplishments, even to those that have never had your best interest in mind. Negative people tend to keep up to date statuses on those in which they feel they can never defeat. That is all due to whom they are and the type of person that they have become. Don't be afraid of losing people. Be afraid of losing yourself by trying to please those around you. It is never vital to let people know what you are constantly doing. You do not have to prove anything to anyone but yourself. You should be your only competition, relentlessly outdoing yourself.

Keep in mind that the only people mad at those making moves are those standing still. So be prepared to deal with many false friends and true enemies with your success. Success usually comes at a high price of weeding people out of your life. Be conscious of who you are and proud of your personal accomplishment. You being a fan of yourself in a modest manner is all that will count in the end. You should never be bogged down with attempting to prove anything to anyone. Your personal growth and learning experiences from each milestone that you conquer is the success within itself. Don't expect everyone to be excited about what God is doing in your life.

Do not be motivated by the negativity of others but by passion from within. Live, learn and move forward in all that you do. Keep in mind that the only person that you are better than is the person you used to be. Go where your energy is reciprocated, celebrated, and appreciated. Note to self: you have to do this for you. This is for you. This isn't about anybody. Live for you. Honor you. Never lose sight of that. People who don't respect your growth have to go. You inspire people who pretend to not see you; trust me. Women with purpose and goals have no time for drama. They invest energy in things that add value, not only to their lives, but to the lives of others.

Woman to Woman: You know why strangers support you more than friends and family? It is because people who are from the same place as you have a hard time accepting that you have grown, and they are still in the same place. Keep in mind, you don't have to send any of those people an update on you. As Kendrick Lamar would say, "Sit down, be humble." I had to learn that success will make its own noise. I didn't have to go back and remind anyone of anything. I didn't have to say I was a doctor; I was this.... I make that. They already had an idea. As I mentioned previously, at a young age, I was very sure of the type of woman I wanted to be. Many people took this as being arrogant or what people would say as snobbish or stuck-up. Those around me didn't know why I aimed so high. I set my sights on goals early on that many people didn't pay attention to, however, as I started to accomplish those goals, those same people who called me out for being ambitious, started to slowly resurface. I didn't have to update them on not one accomplishment. They were already aware. They kept up with what I was doing via association with mutual associations or family. Those very people who doubted and ostracized my goals and dreams are now able to figure how the girl who came from the same place as them, can end up with results so differently. Remember about the previous chapter about mastering one's craft? That worked for me, so I can write about it now.

QUOTE OF THE DAY:

Change the world. And when you've done that, change it again.

– Shonda Rhimes

Day 11

The Key to Keeping Your Balance Is Knowing When You've Lost It.

Your brain creates your reality based on where you direct your energy. Life can sometimes feel like one big balancing act. Find the balance between being open-minded but closed off to nonsense. The better you prepare yourself, the better chance of regaining your balance after you lose it. As women, it is important that we learn how to manage and focus on things that can improve our lives. We must stop over thinking failed scenarios, feeding self-doubt and seeing the good in everyone but ourselves. Remember, that you deserve more than that. Energy is so important. It can manifest so quickly just by sitting in our sub-conscious. Sometimes, you must zone out and look internally. Sometimes, it's the world, and sometimes, it's you. It is important that we have the self-awareness to take responsibility for the energy that we radiate. You can simultaneously be both a masterpiece and work in progress.

Every day, we wake up with another chance to start over. We all get the same 24 hours. I know life circumstances can be tough and you are thinking, well, it's not that easy. Ideally, when we wake up in the morning, we must illuminate energy and how we react to certain events will direct that energy. Even if you woke up late this morning, the kids are everywhere, and you can't seem to get it together, will you say you had a bad day? Is it fair that you base your whole day of a rough 30 minutes on how it began? You experienced bad moments, however, if you allow those moments to thrive, then you are creating a reality based on those moments and that is a choice. At times, we can get in the habit of allowing moments and small instances to dictate the rest of our day, week, month, or year. You deserve more peace than that. Don't do that to yourself. It is my prayer that when I close my eyes, that the peace is overwhelming. I try not to allow moments of displeasure and disdain to dictate my life. Traffic is bad every morning, why get angry about traffic being bad every morning when I can leave the house earlier to avoid it altogether? Traffic is bad based on the energy that I'm putting into my perception. However, a mere change in my habits could redirect my energy into what I see as an inconvenience.

There is nothing more valuable than a peace of mind. You should be able to get that through the day and not allow it to weigh so heavily on you to the point where your energy is not aligned with positivity and peace. You are the most powerful tool in your life, use yourself wisely. Understand that energy is transferable. We have complete control over what energy to absorb. Don't be that woman that sucks in whatever is presented to you. It is your choice what to do with bad energy; either pass it on or relinquish it and turn it into positivity.

> **Woman to Woman:** I can recall a time when I was laid off for nearly three months. I was about 23 or 24 years old, at the time, and I was terrified. Just a little background: I left a company to pursue a new position where I could grow my career and 6 months later, they told me that they couldn't support my role. However, each day I walked into my office, I felt uneasy. The energy that I was getting didn't align well with my spirit. It was like I was expecting something to happen because I never felt quite comfortable. Some would argue that I allowed my uneasiness to manifest itself and that became my reality. Others would say that it was God giving me a sign of what was to come. In as much, any way you look at it, I was laid off for nearly three months. I took charge of my life.

After crying for a week, I got up every day and had a schedule to apply and interview for jobs. I put so much positive energy and due diligence out in the universe and was sure of what I wanted in my next position. I was adamant about protecting my energy and aligning it properly so that I was able to see lessons out of that phase in my life and not accept defeat. I was ultimately offered a role that jump-started my career in the direction that it's going today. I was humbled by that chapter and very grateful for learning about the power that I had, energy.

QUOTE OF THE DAY:

A lot of people are crazy, cruel and negative. They got a little too much time on their hands to discuss everybody else. I have a limited amount of energy to blow in a day. I'd rather read something that I like or watch a program I enjoy or ride my damn motorcycle or throw back a couple of shots of tequila with my friends.

– Queen Latifah

Day 12

The Weight Of Self-Discipline Is Much Lighter Than That Of Regret.

You get to a point in your life where you have the confidence, you're investing in yourself by mastering your craft, getting rid of dead weight, not allowing circumstances to get the best of you, but you still aren't where you think you should be, and you ask why. You feel that you are at a standstill. It is so difficult to navigate through life sometimes. We feel like we deserve something, and we are overlooked, and life just isn't fair. In essence, we have to trust the process. It is so hard to do so. I know just from my personal experience. As I mentioned in the previous chapter, I was laid off for three months at one time. Nevertheless, that chapter of my life spear-headed my consultant career and inadvertently positioned me exactly where I wanted. We must remember that delay is not denial. During the time in between where you are and where you want to be, you must do your due diligence.

If something feels off, it is. God is protecting you from a situation or warning you of something. Trust the signs, and don't rush. The comparison is a thief of joy. We all have, at one time or another, compared our lives to someone else's. Who are you to compare your chapter 12 to someone's chapter 20? We never know what it took for someone else to get where they are, so we can't compare our life journeys and timetable expectancies. Sometimes, God holds you back temporarily until the road is safe and clear to continue. Be thankful for the stall.

We never know what God is aligning for us while we are doing our part. Everyone has a blueprint that is specifically for them. Each person can navigate in a manner in which they see fit. Some of us have more complex blueprints, while others do not. Neither is a disadvantage. You have to remember that you are built uniquely to prepare you for your life's events. You may not see it today or tomorrow, but you will look back in a few years and be absolutely perplexed and awed by how every little thing added up and brought you somewhere beautiful – or where you always wanted to be. You will be grateful that things didn't work out the way you once envisioned. It will always make sense in the end. At times, we think we are prepared when we are not. Sometimes, God saves us from ourselves and gives us a little more preparation before we can experience abundance. Truth is, when it's your time, nothing will block your blessing. You won't have to do anything but show up because the blessing is reserved especially for you. When you finally get your turn, you will understand why it was worth the wait. Shake off what didn't work out, shake off what somebody told you that you couldn't do. They don't determine your destiny, God does.

> **Woman to Woman:** After completing my doctorate, I decided that I wanted to stay in corporate, but work in the education and change management business unit of my firm instead of the functional and technical side. I had been an adjunct professor for many years and had become passionate about teaching adult learners. After an annual review, I expressed my career goals to my boss. I'm in the field of information technology, and things don't move fast, so I didn't expect to hear anything for a while. A couple of months later, I was interviewed by the directors of that side of the business. Several months went by and things were slow. One morning, unexpectedly, I woke up to an email with an offer. However, it wasn't what I expected. Turns

out, the position that I was interviewed for was given to a guy and they offered me the spot below him. I thought this shot was mine, it was my turn, right? No. I respectfully declined the position. During all of this happening, a colleague from a previous firm had referred me to a recruiter for another position. This position turned out to be even better than the previous one that I wanted. I was interviewed and was offered the job. I didn't do anything but be myself when the time was right. It didn't take any manipulation or finessing; it was all mine. That's how things work in life. When it's your time, it's your time.

QUOTE OF THE DAY:

Never give up, for that is just the place and time that the tide will turn.

– Harriet Beecher Stowe

Day 13

Sit In Your Quiet For A Bit, There Will Be Other Times To Play In Your Loud.

You won't get anything you pray for until you become the type of woman that should receive it. Sometimes, the problem is you. You cannot question anyone's blessing because you feel like you've been short-changed. The question is, when no one is watching, who are you for real? So many of us are guilty of self-sabotaging our future and pointing the finger at everyone else, instead of examining ourselves. Be your best you, instead of emulating who you think you should be. Work hard, release positive energy, and treat others with respect. Stay dedicated to your goals and find different ways to achieve them. Remember, life will happen when you start becoming who you are meant to be, and all the other factors that you thought mattered will be obsolete. Your relationship with yourself will set the tone for every other relationship you have. As you are shifting, you will begin to realize that you are not the same person you used to be. The things you used to tolerate will become intolerable. When you once remained quiet, you will start to speak your own truth. Where you once battled and argued, you will choose to remain silent. You are beginning to understand the value of your voice and there are some circumstances that no longer deserve your time and energy.

Sometimes, you just have to put your head down and do the work. The art of discipline and knowing how to strategically move are both vital. Sitting in our silence allows preparation, discernment, and most importantly, gives us the ability to hone our skills without input from the masses. When we open up, our goals and vision can sometimes be diluted because we have not mentally prepared ourselves enough. Self-evaluation is important in our lives. We must learn when it is time to take a step back and sit in our quiet. It is the human behavior to sometimes manipulate ourselves into thinking that we are doing the best we can when the truth is deep down knowing we can do better. It is critical to keep in mind that half efforts are not rewarded. When it comes to living the life that you desire and growing into your destiny, you must go full fledge. There is no time to waste when your future is at stake.

The best way to accomplish something is to resist the urge to speak about it, while committing to doing the work to bring it to fruition. Don't create a fallacy in your head of entitlement of deserving something you haven't worked for. It isn't easy to see others get things you think you deserve, but you don't know how long or hard that person has worked. Your chapter 4 may be their chapter 30. We all have unique journeys, trial and error are inevitable, but the decision to continuously put your all in your life is a choice. Ask yourself, are you doing what you must do to eventually get the life you desire; to become the woman that you have envisioned? If not, what is stopping you? You! No one has control over your life but You. Life is less about what happens to us and more about how we react to circumstances. Don't allow hardship, challenges or instances deter you. It's easy to say who or what we want to be, the effort is in the action behind those words. Success is a result of dedicated actions. Train your thoughts to produce those things that can make you better. Discipline is key in all that we do. The mind is the most important part of our bodies. The way our thought process works can determine how we see ourselves and what we can do. Sometimes, you have to zone out and look internally. Sometimes, it's the world and sometimes, it's you. Self-awareness is a skill worth practicing. Don't be upset about the results you didn't get from the work you didn't do.

Woman to Woman: Note to self: you can do better! It is amazing how I thought I knew what I wanted. I remember getting so upset with my father because he wouldn't co-sign for the car that I wanted at the time. He told me, "Little girl, when it's your time, you won't need a co-signer." One of the best things he ever had done for me that shaped my outlook on hard work. I wasn't entitled to get that car. It wasn't my time. I had a job, but I could do better. Exposure to higher education, more cultures, and life experiences shifted my life on what I thought was important and broadened my perspective. I learned that I had to move at the speed that was appropriate for my lane. I learned, what I released to the world is donated back to me. I had to realize that not all hustle is heard. Sometimes, it's just you, all alone grinding, elevating, evolving, while no one hears a sound.

QUOTE OF THE DAY:

Find out who you are and be that person. That's what your soul was put on this Earth to be. Find that truth, live that truth and everything else will come.

– Ellen DeGeneres

Day 14

Don't Let Anyone Rent Space In Your Head Unless They Are A Good Tenant.

Pay attention to how you feel after being around certain people. Do you feel inspired? Drained? Motivated? Protect your peace and energy. Guard it with your life. Turn down invitations, cancel plans; it's okay. It's not selfish. Under no circumstances should you allow yourself to suffer around certain people. Why do we dim our light in hopes that other people around us will feel bright? Don't limit your life to people that you understand. Surround yourself with people who force you to level up. If the people around you aren't making you better, then the relationship is pointless. Realize the higher the standard, the smaller the pool; the process of elimination is mandatory. Never dumb it down, make them come up and get it. God knows who belongs in your life and who doesn't. Trust and let go. Whoever is meant to be there, will still be there. Sometimes, spending time away from people and focusing on yourself for a while is just what you need, don't be afraid to dismiss yourself.

The universe does this thing where it aligns you with people, things, and circumstances that match your energy. The higher your vibrations, the more you will attract things and people beneficial to your life. Sometimes, you must temporarily close yourself off to others to maintain your spiritual maintenance. Be disciplined about what you respond and react to; not everyone or everything deserves your time, energy, and attention. Stay in your light. Whoever is trying to bring you down is already beneath you. In a year's time, the people that once hurt you will linger in the same place, mentally, physically, and financially and if your paths cross again, you'll be unrecognizable, due to the glow of your growth, happiness, and self-love. Keep moving forward, there's nothing back there turning around for; stay focused.

It's human nature to forgive. Forgiving brings us internal peace. However, we must stay cognizant of the people we let recycle back into our lives. People are who they are. We as women take on the challenge of thinking we can save everyone. It's in our nature; a gift and a curse. While some people do deserve a helping hand, and can use our help, it's important for us to decipher the wolves in sheep's clothing. Some people are only present if you have something to offer. Some are there with so many issues they become your issues and the relationship becomes draining. Some are there with motives unbeknownst to you. Everyone in the audience isn't a fan. Trust your discernment, don't go against it. After a relationship has ended or withers away, let it. Good things come full cycle.

> **Woman to Woman:** I tried to hold on to a relationship that was no good for me. After years of turmoil and bad energy, I still tried to keep this person in my life. She was my first childhood best friend. However, there was always an issue in our relationship. When we were young, it was just high school gossip. As we grew older, it was looks and hearsay, all that came from her. I never could understand how a person that I loved, and the relationship I valued so much could be so much work. It got to the point that I did not trust her. During one of the toughest events of my life, my parents' divorce, she showed her true colors. She had a lot to say and she meant it. In addition, her actions during this time were beyond my belief. It was almost like she enjoyed seeing my pain. I ended up dissolving the relationship and proceeded with my life. Years later, she and I bumped into one another and reconnected. She was able to express

her perspective and even apologized. I thought about it, her, the conversation we had that lasted nearly two hours that day. It was right there and then that I made a conscious decision to finally come to peace with the relationship and move on. As I said, people are who they are.

QUOTE OF THE DAY:

I will not have my life narrowed down. I will not bow down to somebody else's whim or to someone else's ignorance.

– Bell Hooks

Day 15
Sometimes, We Are Just Collateral Damage in Someone Else's War against Themselves.

When someone doesn't know who they are spiritually, they usually don't have much to offer. You can't expect depth when the focus is on the surface. When relationships disperse, and we can't figure out why, we often try to find blame in ourselves; what we could have done differently. Sometimes, it is about you, and other times, it has nothing to do with you at all. Don't try to change anyone, change how you deal with them. Despite how open, positive, peaceful, and thoughtful you attempt to be, people can only meet you as deeply as they meet themselves. You have to get to a point where your mood doesn't shift based on the insignificant actions of someone else.

I am at a place in my life where peace is a priority. I deliberately avoid certain people to protect my mental, emotional, and spiritual state. I had to learn that everyone can't be a part of my journey. At times, we as women sacrifice so much of ourselves to help everyone else that we drown in our decisions. We must be mindful of who we chose to carry once God has given us clarity. When you are on a mission to find yourself, you will start letting go of those things meant to keep you lost. You won't allow yourself to be enmeshed in what somebody else is. This could be doing things you don't like just because you want to be with or keep someone. You will end up losing your self-worth, who you really are, and before you know it, you will start losing your sense of direction. You will start living someone else's life, instead of being your unique self. If the person happens not to love themselves or in conflict with themselves, you will be the first to receive the hit because they don't have the ability to love themselves let alone loving another genuinely.

You alone have the power to keep yourself from losing the self within you. So, when you find yourself where you are not comfortable with or where your personality is being affected negatively, leave! This usually happens when you feel your life is more dependent on someone else's. And if anything happens, you feel shattered. Learn to be true to yourself, and don't allow anyone dictate how you live your life or you might end up crushed. Never give someone the advantage of being comfortable watching you suffer. Make your peace and move on.

> **Woman to Woman**: When I was in college, I was introduced to a seemingly great guy. We had a long-distant relationship because we went to two different universities. He was on scholarship at a big school and headed for a great football career. I would fly up and go to his games when I could. We instantly connected, and things moved very fast. Before I knew it, we were in a long-distant relationship. Things maintained for a while until he suffered an ACL injury that threatened his football career. While in recovery, his attitude changed, he became a different man right before my eyes. I thought it would pass when he was completely healed. He had played football since he was five. That's all he knew, and it was being compromised. I was supposed to stick it through with him, right? Um…no, I wasn't. Oh, how hindsight is 20/20. He constantly showed behavior that wasn't worthy of my attention. I should have walked away when I saw the signs. When he decided not to turn back to football, he became a different person. I should have walked away. He was in a war internally within and I could do nothing to help him

be the victor. It had nothing to do with me. Thus, by trying to stay around in his life, it brought me so much pain. I watched his life spiral out of control before my eyes. I tried to lure him back to reality, but it was nothing I could do. I compromised my self-respect to slow him down. It took me a long time to get closure from this relationship.

However, one day I looked up, and time had passed and it all made sense. It was my first adult relationship and I hadn't had much experience being committed to someone and understanding the signs to when to walk away. Nevertheless, life went on. Years later, he would face ordeals and only thing I could do was thank God for sparing me from what I thought I wanted. I was just a casualty of his internal war. However, I learned more about myself than I did him. From that point on, I knew what I would never accept again. I made peace with it, life went on…as it always will.

QUOTE OF THE DAY:

Don't compromise yourself.
You are all you've got.

– Janis Joplin

Reader's Reflection:

Day 16

Do Not Just Slay Your Weaknesses; Dissect Them And Figure Out What They Are Feeding On.

Know that test of strength is the easiest part; it is the test of weaknesses we fail most. Your strengths are things you can leverage on to make you more successful in life. On the other hand, your weaknesses are not your downfall but meant for you to improve on. It is not something you lack, but something you need to work on. To leverage on your strengths and improve on your weaknesses, you need to know them first. You can do that by taking some time to think and identify your biggest personal strength which would be something that comes very easily for you, something you are already good at that comes naturally for you that you won't need to invest too much of your time and effort in it.

Sometimes, you will be presented with the same thing packaged differently to see how you react to it. It's so important to find the root cause of your issues. Every action, perspective, idea is rooted from something. Thus, this also has to be true when dealing with weaknesses. In order to understand why you end up with the same results or constantly dealing with the same scenarios, you have to ask yourself what lands you in that position. It's not easy to tear yourself apart to get to the foundation. However, I think it's a pure necessity to truly understand who you are and why you respond to things in the manner in which you do. Mistakes are painful, but as time goes by, it becomes a collection of experiences that we consider life lessons.

To get to your foundation and find out where the cracks are, you have to be brutally honest with yourself. You can fool a lot of people, but you will always be confronted with the same circumstances and it would be like going through a revolving door without an exit. We find it easy to say what others are doing wrong and where their issues lie, however, it is crucial that you take this same initiative with yourself. What are the roots of your insecurities? Why do you find comfort in a certain type of man that you know is no good for you? Why do you put yourself in circumstances to be used? These are all issues that many women deal with. One of the most complicated things about womanhood is that we must correct a lot of perspectives and beliefs that steamed from our childhood. Not to say that our parents did a horrible job, but living as an adult, we know that there isn't a handbook for the journey. Thus, mistakes will be made as many mistakes were made in our adolescent years that force a cause for correction. Healing doesn't mean the damage never existed, it means you are making a sound decision to no longer let the effect of damages control your life.

> **Woman to Woman:** As far as my mind goes back, I have had the sense of independency. I knew that I wanted to be this goal-driven woman with several accomplishments under my belt. I wanted to be able to say that no one helped me become who I was and that I worked hard and as a result, benefited from it. As I transitioned into young womanhood, this perspective came along with me. People would tell me that I always do what I put my mind to and would ask me how and why I stayed dedicated. It wasn't until I had a conversation with my mother years ago that I really understood why. You see, my mom was identified as a wife and a mother. That was her greatest accomplishment. She sacrificed so much of herself, her ambition, and her future to be what she thought we needed. In my teen years, I would see the role she played and would think, I never want to do that. Meaning,

give up who I was just to please someone else. Yes, as a mother and wife, many women do this every day. I always told myself that I will be selfish and accomplish everything that I put my mind to. As a result of being driven by not only purpose, but resentment, I began to isolate myself at various transitions throughout my journey. I had to see my mom, whose identity was based on being a wife and a mother go through depression when she and my father divorced when I was about 24. Though she was still a mother, my siblings and I were all out the house and she felt she didn't have an identity. As a result, I worked harder. Again, going through periods of isolation while holding so much anger and resentment. I would stress out and feel like the world was on my shoulders. I had to get into counseling to get to the root cause of what I thought was an over- ambitious mind. I had to get to the root cause of what I was feeling so I wouldn't self-destruct.

QUOTE OF THE DAY:

Sometimes, you don't realize your own strength until you come face to face with your greatest weakness.

– Susan Gale

Day 17

Every Girl Needs A "We Gotta Get Our Sh*T" Together Friend.

Your journey is not the same as mine, and my journey is not the same as yours, but if you meet me on a certain path, may we inspire and encourage one another. No true friend should support your stagnated state. Be open to developing new relationships. A new friend can have better intentions for you and open your eyes to see your full potential versus someone you knew your whole life. It is your responsibility to cultivate the right relationships that feed on progression and not regression. Don't let opportunities pass you by because you are afraid of leaving someone behind. If you find yourself in a different circle of friends and you are growing from it, you should not feel guilty.

Trust, respect, loyalty, and communication are the four essential parts of any relationship. Someone helping you is not always your friend. Someone opposing you is not always your enemy. A true friendship is two people who refuse to give up on one another and truly have the best intentions in mind. Reactions are our greatest source of wisdom about people. Be aware of how important words are in life and the effect they have on people. A good friend can literally speak life into you when you feel beat up by this cold world.

It is important to have a mentor. I urge you to find someone who you can learn things from without any conditions. It is vital to have a connection with someone that is invested in your growth. A relationship like this will help you through the turmoil that life sometimes brings. We all know the feeling of what it's like to go through something and feel like you're alone. You can't share everything with everyone so it's important to designate a non-conditional person. This means, that nothing is off limits. You can discuss things with this person that you may not feel comfortable sharing with everyone else. For example, if your mate does something and you forgive them. Your friends may not, so that puts you in a position not to want to reveal certain things to them, but you need someone to talk to, your mentor is that person. There are no conditions on how you should feel or what you should do. This person simply listens when you need someone and offers advice from an unbiased point of view.

> **Woman to Woman:** I recall the time I was down to my last thousand dollars. It was my first year in Atlanta and I didn't have work. I was going on interviews and just trying to press forward. I had no friends, no family, just me and my determination. I went to get my hair done so that I could be presentable going on job interviews. I found someone with great work and who I could afford. Never did I know how sitting in her chair would change my life. This is the day I met Joy Stewart. Undeniably the first person to ever call me Dr. Cee, when I was just one semester deep into my doctoral program. I sat in her chair, a broken young girl, ready to just throw in the towel. She told me no. She said my story was worth hearing and how it was my duty to keep pushing so that young girls, like her daughter, could see me thrive and become inspired. She said when I walked in her shop, she saw something special in me and that God had put it on her heart to talk to me. This one encounter with Joy led me to stay in Atlanta and push through. From that point on, she would call and pray with me. She would check on me. She really cared about me and I had nothing to offer her other than

being who I was. She said that she was on the journey of becoming as a well, and we could grow together. From that day on, she has become one of the closest people in my life. My mentor, my big sister, my counselor. She is my "get your sh*t together friend." I am forever grateful for our connection. Now, I have become a mentor to her daughter. You see, God and the universe has a funny way of working like that. He knows when to place the right people in your life. Joy isn't here to be my yes man, but more so, check me if I'm wrong or have clear eyes when my vision is clouded by bias. I definitely know that if I would not have ever sat in her chair, there is a good chance that I wouldn't have gone the right direction.

QUOTE OF THE DAY:

No person is your friend who demands your silence, or denies your right to grow.

– Alice Walker

Day 18

Rather Than Expecting People To Change, Inspire Them To Do So Willingly.

The caterpillar. The cocoon. The butterfly. One thing that I learned is that each season of life is different. As you are coming out of each phase of your life, you can't expect others to grow with you. Your journey is for you and will be understood by those who are meant to grow with you. The thing that you have to accept is that you can't take everyone with you. It is hard to let go, it's hard to let go of a connection that you've shared with someone for years. However, it is not your responsibility to force people to grow with you. You cannot extend your personal expectations on what other people should be. Just like you had to come into your own, it's a process for others as well.

As women, we naturally try to become fixers. We try to fix every situation. We try to fix our children. We try to fix our men or partners. We try to fix everyone or thing we come in contact with because we think we know what's best. Unbeknownst to popular belief, it isn't our job to touch everything we see or are exposed to. You have to let people live, let people be who they are. The hope should be that they become inspired by you as they witness your growth. It isn't your job to judge or take own the responsibility of forcing someone to become who you think they should be. Learn to let people be who they are and accept that. If that person serves you no good, know when to walk away. A person will only change when they are ready. There is nothing you can do or say to affect someone who isn't looking to grow. You will constantly be disappointed and there is no valid reason to do that.

You can't want something for someone more than they want it for themselves.

So many of us go wrong trying to get our mate to be exactly who we think they should be, when truthfully you know who you are dealing with and what you signed up for. A person will always show you who they are. It is up to you to believe it. You can't change that dog. You can't make a father be a father. You can't make a player settle down. You can't force a man to marry you. You can't force someone to commit. Pay attention to who you are dealing with and make a decision if you are willing to grow through things with that person. However, be aware of the risk involved. That person may never grow. That person may never get it. If you are willing to take them on, you have to have the patience to deal with and the discipline to know when you've had enough. Just know that you can't force someone to become who you think they should be. It's never worked and never will.

> **Woman to Woman**: I have learned to accept people at face value. I could have avoided a lot of heartache and disappointment if I had paid more attention to who people actually were versus who I wanted them to be. It took some time, but I got to a place in my life where I become more observant and careful who I dealt with. I became exclusive about who I let in my life and what I put my energy towards. I had a high school and a college friend that I put the wrong trust into. I had to learn from those mistakes. As I began to walk in my truth, I prayed for discernment in all that I encountered. I wanted to know who I was dealing with and what their intentions were. I would ask God to make things clear for me as I embarked on new journeys and relationships. I didn't want to have my guard up, but I didn't want to go through a cycle of mistakes either. It's like, He began to place the right people in my life. The people that took time to understand me. I didn't

have to wear a mask or have explanations because they knew who they were dealing with and vice versa. The goal in all my relationships just is to help one another grow, not to force beliefs or judgements upon each other. I found this first in my sister, Clardia, then in my best friend, Neda also in my sister friends, Ashley, Candice, Crystal, LaToya S., Latoya B., my favorite Sheena, my cousin, Jasmine, and a new relationship that I have formed with others over the years, like with Shennise, LaChara, Jamie, Pe'a, and Kesha. I'm glad that I now have people who accept me and vice versa. The goal isn't to get others to change. It is to become someone that inspires others so that they will find their way through various circumstances. We all need support from other women. There is a commonality between women worth understanding, worth figuring out once the wrong ideals are removed.

Quote of the Day:

My number one way to empower everyone, who are fathers and brothers as well, is to embrace that strength has no gender, we can come together in that.

– Venus Williams

Day 19

We Accept A Lot Of Things But Struggle With Accepting Ourselves, Why?

Take responsibility for all that you are. That gives you the power to become whatever you wish. When you have a warrior mentality, an attitude of faith, then the forces of darkness cannot stop you. There is no comparison between the sun and the moon, they both shine when it's their time. Challenges are what make life interesting. Overcoming them is what makes life meaningful. No matter how much you regret the past, nothing can change it.

It comes naturally for women to have the answers for everyone else, but when it comes to ourselves, we struggle. Reliving past mistakes will never help you grow. It is critical that you accept yourself, flaws and all. Every experience is unique to your growth. You can't be hard on yourself when it comes to mistakes of your past. Things happen. You live, learn, and you grow from it if you are willing. If you continuously beat yourself down, how do you expect to heal? Healing is a huge aspect of growth. It's very hard to come to terms with things of your past, but it's critical to let your spirit have peace.

If you are living and struggling to accept yourself, it becomes visible to others. You leave yourself open to be vulnerable to the wrong type of attention that people may take for granted. We all have been unhappy at some point in our lives. No one's life is perfect. However, the thing about life is that you only get one. It's up to you to decide how to live it. Don't force yourself to live in shame. Don't allow anyone to make you feel guilty about your past. We all have chapters that we don't want anyone to read. You are not the only person that has made mistakes. If you have hurt someone, ask God for forgiveness, then forgive yourself, and finally, ask that person for their forgiveness. What happens after that is up to that person. You have done your part.

> **Woman to Woman:** When I was fifteen years old, I had a hard year accepting myself. I was smart, ambitious, had a solid understanding of what direction I wanted to go in life. However, this was misinterpreted by my peers. I didn't have the luxury of doing a lot of things because my parents didn't want me to grow up too fast. Thus, I had a hard time fitting in because I didn't want to be fast, I didn't want to be boring, I just wanted to be me. However, it wasn't that easy. My peers quickly labeled me as stuck-up because I wasn't doing what they were doing. It wasn't my speed and I was scared of what my parents would think. I was being molded differently. However, it was isolating me. Thus, I began to descend into this phase of trying to be something I wasn't. I know I wasn't a loud show-off. I didn't want to be the center of attention. Fast forward to my junior year, my best friend at the time, the one I mentioned that was toxic earlier, got into a fight with a group of girls. Looking back, I know she was wrong. But what would people say if I didn't help? I had to jump in. I had to let people know I had her back. Well, that escalated quickly and before you know it, I was expelled from school. Every girl involved had to go for a special hearing held by the Board of Education. Just so happened, the day I was supposed to go, there was a bad snow storm that led to my meeting getting cancelled. After my hearing was rescheduled, I was hit with one of the toughest board members who weren't present at my friend's or any of the other girls'

meetings. He told me that it was a shame that I was at the top of my class and involved in such foolishness. He threw the book at me. He told me that he wouldn't expel me because he didn't want it to go on my record because I had a promising future. He proceeded to tell me that I was a follower and I was too smart to have ended up in those circumstances and that I would have time to think about my future while spending the rest of the year out at another school.

Everyone else had a favorable hearing and was allowed to go back and business went on as usual. That experience forever changed my life. I made a promise to myself to always march at the beat of my own drum. How could the best student out of the ordeal end up with the harshest consequences? The answer is simple; I was struggling to accept myself and allowed that vulnerability to be used against me. So, the lesson was simple. If I didn't accept myself, how could I expect others to do so, or respect me?

Quote of the Day:

I didn't learn to be quiet when I had an opinion. The reason they knew who I was is because I told them.

– Ursula Burns

Day 20
Faithin' It!

Don't dig up in doubt what you planted in faith. There's going to be very painful moments in your life that will change your entire world in a matter of minutes. These moments will change you, will test your faith. Let them make you stronger, wiser and kinder. But don't you dare go and become what you are not. Cry if you must. Scream if you must, then you straighten your crown and do what you have to do. Trust the wait. Embrace the uncertainty. Enjoy the beauty of becoming. When nothing is certain, anything is possible.

Challenges are what make life interesting. Overcoming them is what makes life meaningful. If you are going to rise, you might as well shine darling. Your mind is the most powerful tool in your life, use it wisely. You must be aware of how important words are in life and the effect they have on others. Discipline your mind to create positive outcomes, where your tongue becomes an asset and not a liability. Words are powerful. Be who you are created to be, and you will set the world on fire. What will make your story a success is not how hard the troubles were, but how you learned from each experience and overcame them.

Never stop believing that it could happen for you. You don't need to have it all figured out to move forward. Just take the first step. Do the work, keep the faith, be a good person. Sometimes, God presents us with an opportunity and we see it as an obstacle. Believe in yourself and don't talk yourself out of a blessing that is destined specifically for you. Don't settle for less just because it is available. Living guilty and condemned is not going to make anything better. Drop it and step into the new things God or the universe has in store for you. Staying inspired makes every other success possible.

> **Woman to Woman:** Since I could remember, I wanted to go to law school. I wanted to become an attorney. No one in my family had ever gone that far and I wanted to be the first to do so. I went to undergrad on scholarship and did okay. I was arrogant enough to believe I could still pull off being on top naturally and not really studying. After almost losing my scholarship first semester of freshman year, I soon realized that I could not have the same habits; I quickly pulled my act together. Fast forward to senior year, I'm a B student. I was working my butt off to get my GPA to move because I became aware of what it took for me to get into law school. I took a LSAT study course that demanded me to drive to another city every Tuesday and Thursday after class. I was determined to increase my LSAT score. I had to get into law school. I started applying to every law school where I thought I could get accepted during my senior year. I applied to ten schools. I was wait-listed to five, denied by four, and admitted to one. That one yes was all I needed. I had faith that my diligence and hard work would pay off. I know that nothing in life comes easy. However, I have learned how to keep the faith and remove doubt. Staying determined and working diligently makes a world of difference when you have faith. The thing is, when it was my time, nothing could be done to disrupt what was meant for me.

QUOTE OF THE DAY:

Keep your dreams alive. Understand that to achieve anything requires faith and belief in yourself, vision, hard work, determination, and dedication. Remember all things are possible for those who believe.

– Gail Devers

Reader's Reflection:

Day 21

You're Going To Piss A Lot Of People Off By Doing You And Getting Yours; Do You Anyway.

Sometime, somewhere, you will have to hurt someone's feelings on your way to the top for not giving a second thought to their opinion or overly-dramatic feelings. Some people use weapons in the name of "help" to keep others down, and how these weapons are presented as though they "care." It is your sole responsibility to decide whether you want to be pulled down by such feelings or stick up for yourself while climbing up the ladder.

The climb to the top includes stepping on a few toes. No one great ever got anywhere without stepping on any toes, it could be the person competing with you for the job, your father who doesn't agree with your career path or your friend who is jealous of your achievements. There will always be someone in the way deliberately trying to bring you down or just blocking your view. The best way to accomplish something is to resist the urge to tell others about it while dedicating yourself and putting in the work that it demands to bring to fruition.

To achieve your dreams in life, you will have to learn how to piss people off, especially those standing in your way, and stop succumbing to their sentiments. When you're in a situation and it's you or someone else, that person's feelings or yours, your time or someone else's, sometimes, you just need to stand your ground and say you are choosing You. The day you stop caring about what other people think and start caring more about how you feel is the day you blossom into becoming who you're destined to be. And trust me, if they have your best interest at heart, they'll get over it. If they are true friends, they will understand that sometimes, we need to be selfish, sometimes, we can't worry about their feelings before our own. It's your life; you shouldn't have to spend it tiptoeing around people.

Life is hard, rough and not for the weak. It's for those who know how to play the game and finish strong. It's not about how nice you can be and how many toes you can avoid stepping on, it's about getting what you need to get done and refusing to waste your time with insignificant feelings. Life isn't about the number of people you disappoint, but the number of times you were strong enough not to care and go after what you want. Time is the most valuable thing you have, don't waste it doing things you don't want to do. Don't allow those who try to squash your dreams have their way. Admit it; you're a bomb ass woman. Stop pretending you're less than you are to protect someone's ego.

> **Woman to Woman:** I remember when I was younger, I would tell people that I wanted to go to college and then continue to law school. My parents believed in me, but so many people around me, family and so-called friends, thought that I was aiming too high. Though no one ever said it directly, the looks that I would get when expressing my goals showed it all. I was just a little black girl, from East Nashville, who was I to aim high? However, I always knew and felt that I had a purpose bigger than what a lot of people would understand. I had a cousin that was my absolute best friend growing up. She was a couple of years older than me and we were very close in our youth. After graduation, she went on to become engaged and have a daughter. I proceeded to college. Freshman year, I would call her, she was always too busy with her kid or

fiancé. Naturally, as time passed, we grew apart and lost touch. Years later, I saw her at our grandmother's house for Christmas. She gave me the nastiest look and didn't even bother to speak. I was clueless. Of course, information got back to me regarding her discontentment towards me. Apparently, I went to college and forgot all about her. Suddenly, I was arrogant and self-centered. This shocked me. I thought to myself, I called her for a whole year, asked her to come visit me in college, tried to visit. However, she was too busy with her fiancé and son. Thus, I moved on. At the time, I was enrolled in law school. I later found out that she had split from her fiancé and was in a rough patch in her life. I thought about that and concluded that I represented what was once her dream. At a deeper level, it wasn't about me, it was truly about her disappointment with herself. However, I know that I tried to maintain our relationship at one point. I went on with my life and so did she. How was I wrong for continuing to accomplish my goals? That was the first taste that I got of pissing people off by doing what is best for me. I knew deep down that I had never personally done anything to my cousin, we just ended up on different sides of the tracks. To this day, we have never spoken again. My mother told me to be the bigger person, and I told her that if I was the one with the issue, I would. However, under these circumstances, it's personal issue that my cousin would have to deal with.

QUOTE OF THE DAY:

You can write me down in history with hateful, twisted lies, you can tread me in this very dirt, but still, like dust, I'll rise.

– Maya Angelou

Day 22

Girl, You Have To Make Bad Days Look Pretty!

We all have bad days, and some are much worse than others. A really bad day can leave you very devastated and drown in worries. It makes you believe you are crushed and can never rise again. Although not every day is good, there is something good about every day. You must be strong to see the positive side on down days. It takes all those down moments to teach you how to truly appreciate what you have. You don't have to be hard on yourself. If you have made a mistake, learn from it and proceed with life. Cry, if you want to, but never allow the situation to weigh you down, take a deep breath and take corrective action. Sometimes, you need those tears to wash your eyes, so you can see the possibilities in front of you with a clear vision again. Never worry about what you know you can't control.

You are free to make whatever choice you want but are not free from the consequences of the choice. The way up requires some amount of pain. Learning to endure such pain while you climb higher makes you stronger. Don't allow the pain to take the best of you. Successful people don't give up easily no matter the challenges confronting them; they are always resilient. If you want to be successful in life, avoid negativity.

Many times in life, we forget how much we have to be grateful. We only see the pain and the lack and become very sad not taking the time to see how much good we have in our lives and the need to be happy. Let's change our attitudes regarding how we perceive things, and always learn to see the good side of everything responsible for our down moments. When you find yourself down, refuse to remain at that level. Get up! Start over again! Don't forget the "I can" attitude. Confess positively amidst that depressing moments and show yourself some love to preserve you for the good times. Don't allow the pain of life upset all your great plans and big expectations. Know that the situation is temporary, and it will help you cope with whatever you're going through.

> **Woman to Woman:** There was a day I had a terrible confrontation with my ex-best friend. It left me feeling like a victim with all kinds of regrets. I allowed her negative opinion to hurt me and make me feel everything was my fault. I felt the backstabbing pains of betrayal. When I discovered the situation was beginning to weigh me down, I immediately snapped out from it. I told myself that I won't allow anyone not worth being in my space to take my joy and happiness from me. I can't give her that power over me. I decided to start a new direction in my life and was grateful for it all because it taught me what I really wanted and what was important in my life. I lived through it to find a much saner and happier life with people who genuinely love me for me.

QUOTE OF THE DAY:

You have to count on living every single day in a way you believe will make you feel good about your life - so that if it were over tomorrow, you'd be content with yourself.

– Jane Seymour

Day 23

Never Decrease Who You Become So That Others May Feel More Comfortable Increasing Themselves.

If you are constantly adjusting so that others may feel comfortable, it's time for a self-checkup. Many women spend their lives trying to please people (including family, friends, spouses etc.) and make this their main aim in life at the expense of their own wishes. Pleasing others means you start to forget how to say, "No". If you try, you'll feel guilty. This happens when you believe that a good person thinks of others more than themselves. Well, yes up to a point, but you must create a balance where you continue to think of others but give your own wishes and desires higher priority. When this balance tips over so you feel like your whole life is controlled by your need to please everybody, the result is not only stress and unhappiness but low self-esteem. Self-esteem means valuing yourself, and that means being your own friend. When you weigh up your own needs against those of others, you will understand that you simply cannot please everybody.

Trying to please everyone is tied into the fear of rejection and the fear of failure. But the biggest failure in life is failing to be yourself. And the biggest rejection in life is rejecting you. Making others comfortable around you all the time at the expense of your own happiness and progress in life, can give you a victim mentality and that is no good for you or for others. Once you become a victim, when you try to do things for others, you will feel resentful and this will give you low self-esteem. Because those very people you wanted to admire, respect, and love you now reject you, you tell yourself that you cannot be a lovable person. In desperation, you increase your people-pleasing behavior, and this leaves you feeling disappointed and ashamed of who you have become.

Putting your own needs first does not make you selfish because if you do not look after yourself, you can't be a good partner, wife, parent or whatever. You cannot love others without first loving you. You must learn to say NO and to stand up for yourself to help boost your self-confidence too. You need to look for your own approval. What is more important, what others think of you or what you think of yourself? It is time you become your own best friend. You need to start taking care of YOU, and you can't do this without self-acceptance. Be happy with who you really are and then you can learn to like that person. Set your own boundaries so that you can allow yourself time to fulfill your needs and allow that balance between saying NO and helping others to develop, and stick to them. Decide what your priorities are and stop playing the victim. No matter what your past has contributed to your need to please people, you can change. Your new attitude will bring more happiness, confidence, and self-esteem into your life and you'll be a more balanced person.

> **Woman to Woman:** There was a time in my life that I had to deal with a toxic person in my life that was hard to get rid of because I was very attached to him and had invested so much, including my time in him. I kept receiving the blames for every misunderstanding we had just, so I would not lose him, and mostly because I feared loneliness. I thought that it showed loyalty by sticking around because, so many people had abandoned him. Every time he was around, I felt sad, alone, and thought about how I got in so deep. I prayed to God for the discipline to rid myself of the poison that was in the form of this man. One day, I called his phone and it was disconnected. I called for about a week straight. Nothing. I looked up and time had gone on, I was back to myself.

Fast forward to almost ten years later. I got a text message from an old college friend. This guy had made the news for a serious offense. Not to mention, he was on baby number five. The first thing that came to my mind was thank you God for saving me. I was able to break away from him and learned to love myself and become my own best friend. It was then I discovered that I made the right decision for not allowing myself to repress to make someone important. If he acts like a dog, he's a dog. It wasn't my job to reduce who I was as a woman to make him feel like a man. I am thankful for all the past versions of me and making the conscious decisions to love myself deeply.

QUOTE OF THE DAY:

When I dare to be powerful -- to use my strength in the service of my vision, then it becomes less and less important whether I am afraid.

– Audre Lorde

Day 24

Before You Talk, Listen. Before You React, Think. Before You Criticize, Wait. Before You Pray, Forgive. Before You Quit, Try.

As women, we fall into the temptation to treat conversation like we're in a competition. We find ourselves talking and coming up with many stories, all to support our point of view or display our superior knowledge. When you talk, you give away information often more than you intended. But when you listen, you receive information that could be of benefit to you. The truth is when you say less, the smaller the chances you'll share information and later wish you hadn't. Too much talk can make you look less intelligent than you are, and you will minimize the chances of it happening if you listen more than you speak. Most people go through life wishing to have listen more. So, by listening rather than talking, you are giving something valuable to the person who's speaking. It's a powerful relationship-building tool that you should maximize. In the same vein, it's very important for each of us to think before we immediately react by thinking through the various possible intended and unintended consequences of our actions. Always resist the urge to react or respond immediately without letting the words that are being spoken, communicate with you freely. You block communication when you have a premature outburst either in your mind or aloud. Sometimes, you realize that you were thinking about the situation incorrectly or may have overreacted altogether. Other times, you realize that your thinking was right on track but that you may need to figure out your next steps. Giving yourself even a few extra seconds before reacting can make a difference. It puts the power into your own hands to make good decisions and take control of your life.

Before you criticize anyone, ask yourself what you intend to achieve by such act. If your criticism will end up leaving someone more devastated than you met them, then don't criticize at all. Life is too short to spend it upsetting people. Offering to criticize when asked by someone who respects your opinion, is very different from picking holes in someone who didn't ask for your unsolicited advice. If you have to be critical about someone or their work, at least provide some helpful answers. Don't be too fast to criticize because it can be painful, so it pays to wait and think what you aim to achieve before you criticize.

Moving on with your life is difficult unless you are prepared to forgive. Unforgiveness has a way of standing on your way to progress. It can be difficult at times to forgive someone who has hurt you so badly, especially if it's coming from someone you trusted. Sometimes, situations like that happen for you to learn from it. It's pointless to hold bitterness toward people as it has a way of preventing you from being at your best. Always see the positive side of every situation, look for the learning, use it as a lesson; don't let it happen again and move on. In my experience, people tend to quit too soon. Stories of success are ultimately stories of people who didn't give up. When they fall, they rise and keep trying till they get what they want. Don't quit because it seems not to be working the way you expected it. Most times, the reason you never succeeded with your plans was that you quit unreasonably too early. If you are going to try something, really try and try with commitment based on realistic data – then stick to it.

Woman to Woman: There is an art to learning to listen. Not to respond, but to actually listen to what someone has to say. Especially if you have made them feel less than. I had to learn it's not about things I've said, however, that my delivery was pretty awful. A person will never forget how you made them feel. It is important to remember the power of the tongue and how powerful words are. Once you put them out in the universe, they start to manifest. It is your duty to take charge of your words. I had to learn in moments of anger, it is better that I not say nothing at all versus saying something that I could never take back. don't be so critical of others. I learned so much when I decided to be quiet and hear others out and not just looking to respond. I never wanted to be that woman that could dish it and couldn't take it. I know that in order to be forgiven, I had to learn to forgive. In order to be heard, I had to listen. It's not all about how I feel, it's about the impact that I have on others. I had to learn from my mistakes and continue to push through. Even with my best intent in mind, I've been guilty of hurting someone's feelings as well. I had to learn to acknowledge my errors before I criticized someone else. In the moments where I can't gain clarity on my own, I just take it up to God. Every day is trial and error.

QUOTE OF THE DAY:

Life is an opportunity, benefit from it. Life is a beauty, admire it. Life is a dream, realize it. Life is a challenge, meet it. Life is a duty, complete it. Life is a game, play it. Life is a promise, fulfill it. Life is sorrow, overcome it. Life is a song, sing it.
Life is a struggle, accept it. Life is a tragedy, confront it. Life is an adventure, dare it. Life is luck, make it. Life is life, fight for it!

– Mother Teresa

Day 25

Your Past Was Learning, Your Future Is Growing, and Your Presence Is Living.

One of the ways to have a fruitful journey in life is to continuously put your past with painful memories behind you so that it will not affect both your present and future in a negative way. Learning to overcome issues and to be your best self is a constant process. In the same vein, learn to accept your past, embrace your present and what's to come. How you handle your past, determines the way you'll live your present which in turn affects your future. Learning to accept your past is a process, and isn't always easy, particularly if it was traumatic or heartbreaking. Accepting your past is not about wanting to change or forget about it; it's about altering your perception of it so that you can live more freely. Sometimes, events do not just happen; they are programmed for a reason. They are meant for you to learn from it and apply what you have learned in a positive way for the good of your future.

The moment you begin to accept the past, the moment you begin your healing journey. It becomes the start of letting go, moving on, and living more for the present. It is not an easy process, because too often, we find ourselves being taken out of the present moment, and our heads get cluttered with the mind chatter of yesterday, broken memories, and anxieties and fears of what's to come. Whenever you find yourself like this, snap out of the past by taking a deep breath and focusing on your breath; and look past the beauty and simplicity of the present. Harboring your emotions, particularly the negative ones, only brings more emotional turmoil and keeps you stuck in the past.

Entertaining fears and anxiety toward the future come when you neglect your present and hold onto your past. So, in order to enjoy your future, you must first learn to enjoy your present! You can decide to share how you're feeling with someone close to you, whether it's a friend, family member, partner, or therapist; and if you don't have anyone close enough to do this with, let your emotions out through a non-verbal means. This could mean engaging your mind with something you like doing like playing some of your favorite songs, going for a massage, etc. Being in nature can also pull you back to the present moment. Take half an hour out of your day to go for a walk and appreciate nature. Our thoughts create our reality. Be aware of your thoughts so that you manifest a positive reality, not one that's full of struggle.

> **Woman to Woman:** It took me years to learn how to live presently. Like I earlier shared about my parents' divorce which was very traumatic for me, especially because I watched my mother going through so much pain and suffering because of that experience. I was filled with bitterness against my father. I least expected he would be the source of heartbreak to us all. I was really devastated. My major fear was for my mother's health. I was worried that she might never be the same. Because of the intense experiences and emotions from my past, it was easy for me to slip back into old ways of being, repeat similar experiences in my life, go around in circles—and essentially miss the present. I had a habit of trying to fix things and be everything to everyone, I was embittered against my father because I couldn't get him to reconsider and stick with my mom. I was embittered because I couldn't be the husband my mom lost, I couldn't be the man my mom needed. Then, I realized that was draining me. Not until I decided to accept

what has happened and moved on, was I free. I decided to take charge and take care of her without losing myself in the process, without letting the situation weigh me down. I decided to live the moment and not allow the past to affect us. Today, we are happier and living with no regrets. I have learnt that I could only be myself while I give others enough to "fill" themselves and not drain me.

QUOTE OF THE DAY:

There are still many causes worth sacrificing for, so much history yet to be made.

– Michelle Obama

Reader's Reflection:

Day 26

You Gotta Learn When To Chill And Recharge.

The quality of your preparation determines the quality of your performance. Progress is a process and you can't be so hard on yourself. Think about it. Everything you do takes time. Going to the salon, getting the kids ready for school, finding the right partner, building your career, etc. You won't be able to change overnight. When you feel the weight of the world on your shoulders, know when to step back and charge up. You can't allow yourself to run around on a drained battery. You aren't good to anyone this way, most importantly, yourself.

The most important thing is the self-improvement you are undergoing. Personal growth is not a day thing. You didn't just grow overnight; the same way it is on your way to be the best you can be. What matters is that there is a change from old you to new you, including your attitude towards life. What you focus on changes everything. Don't look back when you know you shouldn't. Don't stress over unimportant things. Keep looking at the target destination and remain positive. Your attitude directly determines how well you live your life. You simply can't live a positive life with a negative attitude. The road will definitely be rough; you will be faced with obstacles. But remember not to allow the mental blocks control you. Confront your negativity and turn the mental blocks into building blocks. The trick is to be grateful when your mood is high and graceful when it is low.

We will all get there; but while we are striving to get there, let's not forget to always count our blessings and make our blessings count too. It's okay to know that you still have work to do but you have to be grateful on how far you've come. There's no good reason why you must settle for anything less than the very best life has to offer. Start now by sincerely appreciating the things you have and making the most of them. Happiness and success in life are not the byproducts of limitless resources and a state of mind. Take everything as a lesson learned. Keep this in mind, and live it accordingly. Be thankful for where you are now and where you are heading to.

> **Woman to Woman**: I had to learn that I can't be everything to everyone. I've always been a strong and independent person. This somehow gave people the false reality that they can always depend on me. I didn't want to let people down. However, I realized that the very same people that I was there for continuously, never asked me one simple thing, *how are you doing?* People would call me and immediately jump into their issues. Not even considering if I was okay. What if I had a bad day? What if I wanted to rant? I had a detailed conversation with my best friend, she said this is because I always seem to be okay and have it all together. I told her that that wasn't the case, no one just ever asked. She was shocked that I felt that way. However, I had to also take responsibility of not stepping back to recharge myself. I let people drain me without saying anything. I thought all these people needed me. Nevertheless, if I wasn't in the right state of mind, I know that I can't be good to anyone. Over the years, I have learned to stay away from people or things that drain me. I had to tell myself, it's okay to walk away. Some people would consider this to be selfish, I consider this self-awareness of knowing when I need to step away and recharge. People will drain you dry if you give them the opportunity. Sometimes, you just have to excuse yourself gracefully from the circumstances.

Quote of the Day:

When you take time to recharge, you are more effective and productive.

– Arianna Huffington

Day 27
Discover Your Truth.

Never not walk in your truth again. Inside you is a person waiting to jump out and live in truth and openness. It means living to be who you are and not someone different. "Your truth is rooted in your belief system; it's the things you feel and say to yourself behind your public mask." It is about not spending your days living up to someone's expectations and definitions but yours. But here lies the issue like someone said, "Because within each of us, there is a gap between our truth and the person we show to the world. How wide that gap may be will depend on our level of self-awareness and the layers of filters and fictional stories about who we are that we've built up over the years. This happened because it is in our human nature to want to be accepted, which often put much pressure on ourselves to fit in ... or at the very least, to not stand out in a way that makes us feel exposed or foolish; so, we end up masking or manipulating our most vulnerable feelings, beliefs, and desires in an effort to avoid judgment, discomfort or rejection."

The challenge is that we are rarely consciously aware of our efforts to protect and disguise parts of ourselves, which means that before you can learn to live your truth, you have to muster the courage to dig down and uncover the real you behind your filters. Of course, after years of disguising vulnerabilities and artfully crafting fictional stories, it may take some work to get to know the real you and begin slowly closing that gap ... and the truth is that, sometimes, we harbor a fear that we may not like what we find all that much. So then, is it worth it? If you're relatively comfortable now, what could possibly be gained by putting yourself through this exercise in self-discovery? There is nothing more powerful than a jumble person with a warrior spirit who is driven by a bigger purpose. How miserable it must be for those living their lives in accordance to the standards of everyone but their true self. To wake up every day and force oneself to do something that you don't want to do; putting on a mask to appease everyone but yourself. That would be like never waking up from a nightmare.

It's important to understand that learning to live your truth isn't about changing or "fixing" you, it's about freeing you to be the confident, powerful person you were meant to be, and honoring that truth through actions and communication with others, as well as yourself. Living your truth again will better prepare you to handle adversity with a strong sense of Self which helps to enhance your resilience and enables you to face challenges with a more balanced outlook regardless of what happens. When you live your truth, you won't need others to validate worth. You'll have the confidence to speak your truth because no matter how hard you may try, you're never going to satisfy everyone, and it's an illusion to think otherwise. Being authentic in the way you communicate your feelings and perspective is a core attribute of living your truth. Identifying, understanding, and defining your personal truth is one of the most important things you'll ever do in this life. When you show up to a new room, makes sure it's you who shows up. Rock with what you have inside. Live the real YOU.

Woman to Woman: When I was a teenager, I had a hard time finding my truth and living it. I was pretty focused, and people interpreted that for arrogance. I just knew it had to be more in the world versus what I was being shown every day. However, I wanted to fit in. I didn't want to be an outsider. Thus, I befriended someone who was completely opposite of me. She was fearless and did all the things that I didn't want to do or wasn't willing to do. She knew a lot of people and had parties, that wasn't my thing but being her friend made it easier for me. She and I never really had too much in common. I was the stylish quiet girl and she was the well-known girl. Thus, we were able to feed off one another's energy. I never realized how toxic she was until years later. Because I didn't walk in my truth, I endured years of a toxic friendship due to the fear of not having one. When I found my truth, I knew that I could never lie to myself again about who I was and who is worthy to be in my life. Now, as a woman, I am who I am. If something doesn't fit me, I simply excuse myself. I refuse to ever be that teenager that I once was, not walking in my light, not walking in my truth. I used to be self-conscious of how other people perceived me because I didn't want to be judged. I knew how that affected me. But, I came to realize that people will judge you whether you are doing good or bad, so I have no choice but to live my best life meant for me. This is the wisest decision I took that contributed to my growth in life today.

QUOTE OF THE DAY:

Be true to what matters to you, and
chase the things that matters.

– Anne Shoket

Day 28
Let Go Or Be Dragged!

*Specially written by J. C. Stewart

How many scars did we justify just because we loved the person holding the knife? How many more stabs will you take before realizing that the person holding the knife does not mean good for you? You can't tell me it was love controlling both of you; you at one end of being stabbed and the person on the other end, holding the knife and stabbing you. Over time, we tend to bend with the rules to avoid the forsaken loneliness that many of us fear. This is where self-love comes in. Why should I remain with someone who obviously is hurting me, who doesn't have my best interest at heart for silly reasons I can't tell?!

Life can come at us hard and fast, and some of the blows can have you ducking and dodging but nothing quite takes the wind out of a woman's sails like heartbreak. There is no other display of emotion that can completely derail your life like a broken heart. The passion and energy that it takes to give yourself over to loving and trusting someone is unparalleled to anything else in the world. To be in love is such a beautiful journey, the butterflies, the anticipation, the feeling of security and trust. However, what do you do when you feel that your love has been taken for granted? How do you push past the pain and recover when you feel that you have been betrayed by your loved one? The grief is unimaginable and stifling to even the most resilient of us. Quite often, we make decisions based on emotions and we subject ourselves to allowing people in our lives that are not nurturing to our souls, they only provide us with instant gratification. Relationships are not perfect, and neither are people, however, your mate should never make you feel less than or emotionally exhausted. You deserve to be with someone that values who you are and the gifts that you bring into the relationship. You should be equally challenging each other to level up and reach higher heights, after all, iron sharpens iron! Your mate should enjoy your company and make time for you, in other words, you teach people how to treat you, and once you have realized that you're not getting treated like you're supposed to, you must let go, and of course, this is no easy feat. This is the hard part, the challenge here is accepting responsibility for your own happiness and understanding that the walking away only shut the door to negative energy and opened the door to invite in a person that really has your best interest at heart.

To truly begin to heal, you first have to forgive, then release, after you release, you reposition your perception. Forgiving someone that has broken your heart is tough, it's so much easier to be bitter, and petty. The fiery embrace of revenge will almost definitely be a most comforting place, but don't let it fool you, it's only temporary, for if you give yourself over to anger, the damage could potentially be an action you can't take back, and in some cases, alter your life permanently, and it's just not worth it. A more positive approach is to let it all out, release it! Cry! Yell! Scream! Curse! And when you are done, forgive them, and yes! You're right, it's absolutely easier said than done, however, forgiveness has a super powerful effect, in that as soon as you do it, that energy has an obligation to catapult you into an even better place emotionally. Once you have forgiven, then you release them, understand that in order for you to grow, you have to face opposition, evaluate the relationship with truth. Be honest with yourself about your role, did you diminish yourself? Allow them to disrespect you? Keep silent when you should have spoken up? Were you selfish? Take some time to work out the answers and then forgive yourself, see the lesson and release the pain. Now comes the best part, repositioning yourself. Don't see a breakup as a failed relationship or a huge mistake, but more so, a lesson that will only make you better. If there was ever a time to be selfish with yourself, this is it. Take a break, go on a vacation, take a couple of days off. Change the scenery, get away from the scene of the crime so you can see everything with fresh eyes. Pray, meditate, try something new. Get back to being the super nova you were before they came along. Always know that they were a star in your universe, not you a star in theirs. You were made fearfully and wonderfully, and the best is yet to come. Have a girl's night! Just make sure that you're participating in productive, forward, self-encouraging activities and stay away from self- deprecating, unproductive, destructive situations that could hinder your healing. You got this. God did not create you to be a blanket to be dragged around carelessly for another's enjoyment. You are a designer original, one of a kind, and if they could not rise to the occasion and recognize the jewel you are, then let them go, and move forward towards your purpose. Remember, this is just a comma, not a period!

> **Woman to Woman**: I don't know much about algebra, but I know about having a broken heart. I fell in love with the love of my life when I was 23, and my falling was the equivalent of free falling from space. I was all in, he said he was as well. He pursued me for 3 months just for a date. It was so romantic, I just knew he was my soulmate, we could finish each other's sentences, we did everything together, we loved the same music, books, etc. This man knew every inch of my body like, no one before him. Girl! When I tell you, he was amazing in bed, it was an understatement. I mean honestly, I thought I could not have found anyone that loved me more or that I wanted to be with this intensely, so of course, when he asked me to marry him, I was like duh! We were broke, and young with a small child and we had some challenges because we both grew up in the rougher part of Miami. Nothing from his past deterred me from loving him and fully committing myself to be the perfect wife.

When he could not find work, I laid my dreams aside and supported any endeavor he tried. None of them worked, but I never allowed him to feel like he had failed us. I encouraged him and financially kept us afloat whenever he did not make enough, always pushing him to do better. I went as far as creating resumes and basically being a consultant to him to help him get promoted. As he began to climb the ranks, I moved further and further away from my dreams. One day, my world came crashing down and I found out that my husband was having an affair.

Devastation was not the word. I felt betrayed, and desolate. I cried and did not eat for days, and then I started eating everything. The first time, he begged me to forgive him and I did. I counted the cost and I thought I was strong enough to move on. That was not his last affair, and each time I caught him, I had so many questions, like why am I not enough? And he said I was, but his behavior said otherwise. Each time we reconciled, a little piece of me died. By the time we reached the 15th year, the person I knew as Joy was no longer existent, the light I used to have was not dim, it was blown out. I felt so lost, and burdened down with grief. I had no self-esteem at all. I had allowed a very selfish, manipulative person to take up residence in my heart. I had been afraid to fail, and afraid to be alone so long that I was confused. The last straw was a very public affair. Once my family and friends knew, it was out in the open, I had to face it. Truth be told, they always knew but no one spoke of it. It took every ounce of strength I could muster up, but I prayed and asked God to just this one day, give me the wherewithal I needed to walk into that courthouse and file for divorce. I did, it was the most disheartening thing I had ever done. I literally felt like I was grieving a death, I preferred that over this because at least, death was final. During this process, I had to rediscover who I was, and self-examine why I stayed in a toxic relationship that long. It made me reevaluate every single relationship in my life, and I began to clean house. I realized that by lowering my standards and succumbing to low self-esteem, I gave my power over to a selfish energy and taught people to mistreat me. I had to take responsibility for my role in the marriage. Yes, I loved him. Yes, I wanted it to work. Yes, I did not believe in divorce, but I did and still do believe that the Lord wanted great things for me and the pain I was going through was not in His plan. I had to let go of fear and get rid of the negativity. I journaled, I prayed, and I had to forgive him.

The lesson in that is, you can forgive someone, but you do not have to reconcile them back to the previous position in your life. I now know where to place people in my life. If they are selfish, or negative, I don't entertain it, I don't stay in relationships that are not going anywhere. I had to learn to be happy with who I am and understand that everything I needed to be great, was already inside of me. I had to see that loving him was not wrong, but conceding to a relationship that did not bring out the best in me, yet stagnated me was not productive, and not to allow myself to do that again. More importantly, I fell in love again, this time, it was with an amazing person, beautiful inside out, ambitious and resilient, a virtuous woman. I fell in love with myself. I took myself on dates, I spent time with my daughter, and I did things that made me happy. I gave myself a chance to heal and be happily single, and a whole person so that when my Boaz comes along, we can complement one another. This experience, although it seemed to be the most traumatic, the healing process was the best thing I could have ever done for myself.

QUOTE OF THE DAY:

The trouble with some women is they get all excited about nothing - and then they marry him.

– Cher

Day 29
What's Your Story?

You are stronger because you had to be. You are smarter because of your mistakes. You are happier because of the sadness you've known. Now, you are wiser because you learned. No one is perfect. We have, at some point in our lives, done something really stupid that you hope to God no one will bring up ever again. We've all been there. What matters is how it left you, whether weaker or stronger. You become stronger when you learned something from it, and weaker when you did not. Remember, things happen or are allowed for certain reasons. You become wiser when you pick up something to learn from it. In the end, you have reasons to be thankful and happy because you didn't allow yourself to be broken. After all, what are mistakes for, if not to teach us how to act (and not act) in the future? Making mistakes does not define you in any way. From a very young age, we learn through bad decisions like putting your hand on a hot burner, even when warned not to do so, you can bet that you learned to keep your hands away from the burner. Of course, as we get older, mistakes and the lessons we learn from them are more complicated than that. We make career decisions we regret, and bad choices about romantic partners. But we learn from those experiences, too, and become smarter, more mature, and more resilient as a result.

Most times, mistakes made are meant to change you, make you smarter, stronger, and generally more awesome. That is the bitter truth. You can't learn from a mistake until you recognize that it is a mistake—one for which you are responsible. Don't let the fear of failure keep you from trying new things. There is no success without failure, because it opens you to the possibility of creativity and innovation. Your past mistakes must have taught you to know that whenever you have an important decision or choice to make, it's important that you give yourself time to think about your options and the consequences of your actions. Of course, it's impossible to always know if you're making the right choices, but at least, you know you've done your best to do so.

Experience will teach you that you don't beat yourself up for mistakes you couldn't have predicted or prevented. You now realize that, even when you mess up royally, the world continues to turn, and life moves forward. No matter the unpleasant consequences you face, you know that you'll get through it. Don't forget to forgive yourself, and forgive others too. After all, we're only human. Strong women love, forgive, walk away, let go, try again and persevere, no matter what life throws at them.

> **Woman to Woman:** One thing that I had to learn is that everyone won't understand my story because it is meant for me. I have made so many mistakes that I've lost count. I've had toxic friendships and bad relationships that I had to learn from. I have witnessed something that changed my life forever, my parents' divorce. I learned a long time ago that answers to my questions may not come in the clearest forms. However, all these experiences are a part of who I am. We are all products of our experiences. It is what we decide to do with those that define our story. Through the worst moments in my life, when I thought I would never prevail, somehow, some way, God saw fit to keep me going. Now, with more awareness of self and my truth, I am aware that I am who I am. I may have been to the tip of the cliff, but I have never fallen off. That's my story. Challenges that I have prevailed through. Growing to be stronger than I ever thought I was. Being

able to lead by example and inspire those around me with the lessons that I've learned. I am able to thrive today because my story was uniquely designed for me to experience things to get me to this point. As I lived through those issues, I never thought that I would get here, but here I am, living out my story. Walking in my truth.

QUOTE OF THE DAY:

I believe in the power of storytelling. Stories open our hearts to a new place, which opens our minds, which often leads to action.

– Melinda Gates

Day 30
Pay It Forward.

Then it happens, one day you wake up and you're in this place. You're in this place where everything feels right. Your heart is calm. Your soul is lit. Your thoughts are positive. Your vision is clear. Your faith is strong than ever, and you are at peace. At peace with your past, what you've been through and most importantly, where you are headed. Don't neglect things like this. Be kind to others as you are being kind to yourself. While you are working on yourself, try to affect others too in a positive way. We all need that effective turnaround to improve our lives. These small moments of joy will add up and keep you pointed in a positive direction.

It is so important that we learn to help one another thrive. I'm not saying it is your responsibility to dictate someone's life. However, as women, we all share several common experiences. Remove race, ethnicity, social class, careers, and strip us bare. Many of us would have similar stories. The world has divided us in ways I couldn't imagine. Don't let the world harden you. There is so much going on in modern time and every day, there is another unbelievable story that has made headlines. It is so hard not to get discouraged, especially when politics play such a huge role in our daily lives. It is important to not be sucked in to the world wind of chaos. It's enough to see it every day in the world, you don't have to let it live within.

I urge you to take your lessons and share them when they are welcomed. Some young girl out there is about to make your mistakes, help her not to do that. Because you have reached a place of peace, don't become arrogant like you've always had yourself together. The universe has a way of humbling us when our arrogance proceeds. As women, we are a stronger force united than we are divided. Life shouldn't be about competition, more so collaboration. Don't get caught up in the hype of things. Stay true to who you are in the most challenging moments. Once you find your purpose, focus on that every single day. There is internal satisfaction once you know it's not about you. It never was. We are all intricately connected in a way that none of us could imagine. The soul of the woman is like no other. Imagine how powerful we could be if we just took time to get to know one another, withstanding judgement and jealousy. I urge you to get to know someone that you misunderstand. Connect with her to see if an issue can be resolved. Often times, we allow lack of communication or pre-conceived views to destroy a possible connection.

> **Woman to Woman**: I decided to write this book based on my experiences. I'm not advocating that I am an expert. I figured that I can't be the only woman that has been through this. I was so afraid of sharing some of these stories. However, I know that my purpose is to inspire others. For if it were not for those very circumstances, I would have no story to write. My prayer is that someone is touched from this to write their own story. As we become women who've experienced and overcame things, we forget how it once was to be in those circumstances. Thus, it's easy to say, she's this or she's that and judge the next woman. This book illustrates that I've been a complete mess at times. I haven't always had it together. I work daily to walk in my trust and ensure that I'm not disappointing God. Every day is still a challenge. There is a big bad world out there that says I should be everything but myself, I refuse to do that. I want women to know that we are the strongest creatures that have ever been created. We are the bearer of children and literally birthed civilization. I'm amazed at how some women have managed to endure so

much and still push through. Then I remember how I made it through things when there was no light. With women, it's like nevertheless, we persist.

QUOTE OF THE DAY:

If you have knowledge, let others light their candles in it.

– Margaret Fuller

Reader's Reflection: